revolution

revolution

FACES

OF

CHANGE

EDITED BY JOHN MILLER AND AARON KENEDI

THUNDER'S MOUTH PRESS

Published by

Thunder's Mouth Press

841 Broadway, Fourth Floor

New York, NY 10003

Cover and interior design: Big Fish

Library of Congress Cataloging-in-Publication Data
Revolution : faces of change / edited by John Miller & Aaron Kenedi.
p.   cm.
ISBN 1-56025-261-8
1. Statesmen—20th century—Biography. 2. Revolutionaries—20th century—Biography.
I. Miller, John, 1959–   II. Kenedi, Aaron.
D412.R48 2000
920'.009'04—dc21   00-021775

Distributed by Publishers Group West
Printed in the United States of America
10 9 8 7 6 5 4 3 2 1

SPECIAL THANKS TO:

AMY RENNERT

ELEANOR REAGH

MARK JACOBS

BESSIE WEISS

KIM INDRESANO

STEPHANIE HEALD

contents

"We must become the change we envision."

—Mohandas K. Gandhi

che guevara

by Fidel Castro

HE WAS ONE OF THOSE PEOPLE WHO IS LIKED immediately, for his simplicity, his character, his naturalness, his comradely attitude, his personality, his originality, even when one had not yet learned of his other characteristic and unique virtues. In those first days he was our troop doctor. And so the bonds of friendship and warm feelings for him were ever increasing.

He was filled with a profound spirit of hatred and loathing for imperialism, not only because his political awareness was already considerably developed, but also because, shortly before, he had had the opportunity of witnessing the criminal imperialist intervention in Guatemala through the mercenaries who aborted the revolution in that country.

A man like Che did not require elaborate arguments. It was sufficient for him to know that there were

Ernesto "Che" Guevara was born in Rosario, Argentina, where he studied medicine. In 1956 he joined forces with Fidel Castro and laid siege on General Fulgencio Batista's Cuba for three years in an ultimately successful revolution. He served in a number of capacities in Castro's government before returning to the jungles of Latin America and Africa in order to continue the Communist revolution around the world. He was executed on October 9, 1967 by the Bolivian Army and remains to this day a powerful symbol of revolutionary ideals and action.

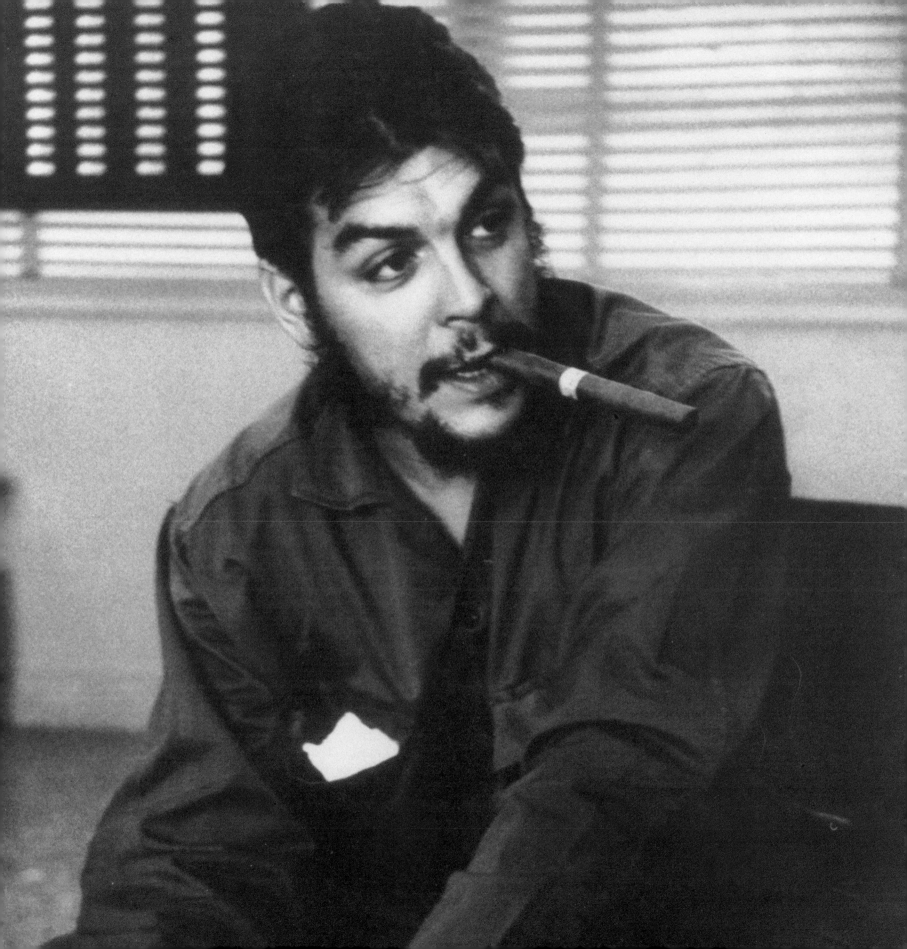

men determined to struggle against that situation, arms in hand—it was sufficient for him to know that those men were inspired by genuinely revolutionary and patriotic ideals. That was more than enough.

One day, at the end of November, 1956, he set out on the expedition toward Cuba with us. I recall that trip was very hard for him, since, because of the circumstances under which it was necessary to organize the departure, he could not even provide himself with the medicine he needed; and, throughout the trip, he suffered from a severe attack of asthma, with nothing to alleviate it, but also without ever complaining.

We arrived, set out on our first march, suffered our first setback and, at the end of some weeks, as you all know, a group of those who had survived from the expedition of the *Granma* was able to reunite. Che continued to be the doctor of our group.

We came through the first battle, victorious, and Che was already a soldier of our troop and, at the same time, still our doctor. We came through the second victorious battle and Che was not only a soldier, but the most outstanding soldier in that battle, carrying out for the first time one of those singular feats that characterized him in all military action. Our forces continued to develop and we faced another battle of extraordinary importance at that moment.

The situation was difficult. The information we had was erroneous in many respects. We were going to attack, in full daylight—at dawn—a strongly defended, well-armed position at the edge of the sea. Enemy troops were at our rear, not very distant, and in that confused situation it was necessary to ask the men to make a supreme effort.

Comrade Juan Almeida had taken on one of the most difficult missions, but one of our flanks remained completely without forces—one of the flanks was left without an attacking force, placing the operation in danger. And at that moment, Che, who was still functioning as our doctor, asked for

> **'I am not a liberator. Liberators do not exist. The people liberate themselves.'**
>
> —CHE GUEVARA

two or three men, among them one with a machine gun, and in a matter of seconds, rapidly set off to assume the mission of attack from that direction.

On that occasion he was not only an outstanding combatant but also an outstanding doctor, attending the wounded comrades and, at the same time, attending the wounded enemy soldiers.

After all the weapons had been captured and it became necessary to abandon that position, undertaking a long return march under the harassment of diverse enemy forces, it was necessary for someone to stay behind with the wounded, and Che stayed with the wounded. Aided by a small group of our soldiers, he took care of them, saved their lives and later rejoined the column with them.

From that time forward, he stood out as a capable and valiant leader, of that type of men who, when a difficult mission is pending, do not wait to be asked to carry it out. . . .

And so it was in combat—in one of the many battles he fought— that he lost his life. We do not have sufficient evidence to enable us to make deductions about what circumstances preceded that combat, to imagine how far he may have acted in an excessively aggressive way, but—we repeat—if as a guerrilla he had an Achilles' heel that Achilles' heel was his excessive daring, his complete contempt for danger.

And this is where we can hardly agree with him, since we consider that his life, his experience, his capacity as a seasoned leader, his prestige and everything his life signified, were more valuable, incomparably more valuable than he himself, perhaps, believed. . . .

It is not easy to find a person with all the virtues that were combined in him. It is not easy for a person, spontaneously, to develop a personality like his. I would say that he is one of those men who are difficult to match and virtually impossible to surpass. But I would say that the example of men like him contributes to the appearance of men of the same caliber.

'Che was the most complete human being of our age.'

—JEAN-PAUL SARTRE

'This man
is bloody
brilliant—
a true
warrior.'

—FIDEL CASTRO

In Che, we not only admire the fighter, the man capable of performing great feats. And what he did, what he was doing, the very fact of his rising, with a handful of men, against the army of the ruling class, trained by Yankee advisers sent in by Yankee imperialism, backed by the oligarchies of all neighboring countries—in itself constitutes an extraordinary feat.

And if we search the pages of history, it is likely that we will find no other case in which a leader, with such a limited number of men, has set about a task of such import; a case in which a leader, with such a limited amount of men, has set out to fight against such large forces. Such proof of confidence in himself, such proof of confidence in the peoples, such proof of faith in man's capacity to fight, can be looked for in the pages of history—but the like of it will never be found.

And he fell. . . .

But those who are boasting of victory are mistaken. They are mistaken when they think that his death is the end of his ideas, the end of his tactics, the end of his guerrilla concepts, the end of his thesis. For the man who fell, as a mortal man, as a man who faced bullets time and again, as a soldier, as a leader, was a thousand times more able than those who killed him by a stroke of luck.

However, how must revolutionaries face this serious setback? How must they face this loss? If Che had to express an opinion on this point, what would it be? He gave this opinion, he expressed that opinion quite clearly when he wrote in his message to the Latin American Conference of Solidarity that if death surprised him anywhere, it would be welcome as long as his battle cry had reached a receptive ear and another hand was stretched out to take up his rifle.

And his battle cry will reach not just one receptive ear, but millions of receptive ears. And not one hand but millions of hands will be stretched out to take up arms.

But he possessed another quality, not a quality of the intellect nor of the will, not a quality derived from experience, from struggle, but a quality of the heart: He was an extraordinarily human man, extraordinarily sensitive.

That is why we say, when we think of his life, that he constituted the singular case of a most extraordinary man, able to unite in his personality not only the characteristics of the man of action, but also of the man of thought, of the man of immaculate revolutionary virtues and of extraordinary human sensibility, joined with an iron character, a will of steel, indomitable tenacity.

And because of this, he has left to the future generations not only his experience, his knowledge as an outstanding soldier, but also, at the same time, the fruits of his intelligence. He wrote with the virtuosity of a master of our language. His narratives of the war are incomparable. The depth of his thinking is impressive. He never wrote about anything with less than extraordinary seriousness, with less than extraordinary profundity—and we have no doubt that some of his writings will pass on to posterity as classic documents of revolutionary thought.

And thus, as fruits of that vigorous and profound intelligence, he left us an infinity of memories, an infinity of narratives that, without his work, without his efforts, might have been lost forever.

And if we speak of sorrow, we are saddened not only at having lost a man of action, we are saddened at having lost a morally superior man, we are saddened at having lost a man of exquisite human sensitivity, we are saddened at having lost such a mind. We are saddened to think that he was only 39 years old at the time of his death.

'I came into close contact with poverty, hunger and disease.... I began to realize there were things as important to me as becoming a famous scientist or doctor: I wanted to help these people.'

—CHE GUEVARA

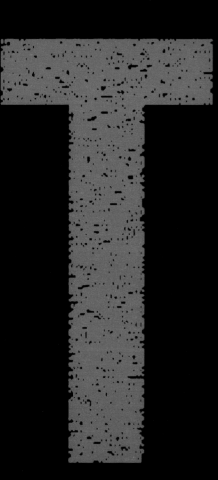

malcolm x

by Alex Haley

IME PASSES SO SWIFTLY, BUT I'M STILL astounded that it really is eighteen years since that Sunday in February 1965: Malcolm X, then thirty-nine years old and known as El Hajj Malik El-Shabazz, had begun to speak in Harlem's Audubon Ballroom when suddenly gunfire erupted and he fell bleeding from multiple wounds. He was rushed to the hospital, where surgeons tried desperately to save him by opening his chest for direct manual heart massage—but soon a hospital spokesperson or somebody told the press and the swelling, weeping, almost mutinous crowd that had kept vigil, "The gentleman you know as Malcolm X is dead." Through the two years before then, I'd been privileged that Malcolm had given me about fifty lengthy and probing interviews to use as the basis of a book chronicling his life. Now and then he would comment that

Malcolm X was born in Omaha, Nebraska. A petty criminal as a teenager, he was sentenced to ten years in prison in 1946 where he taught himself to read and joined the Nation of Islam. He was a powerful speaker and writer, and quickly gained national attention as a leader in the Black Muslim movement led by Elijah Muhammad that preached African-American civil rights should be achieved "by any means necessary." He broke his ties with Elijah Muhammad after his pilgrimage to Mecca. He was gunned down in February 1965 while giving a speech in Harlem's Audubon Ballroom.

'We are not
fighting for
integration...
We are fighting
for recognition
as human
beings.'

— MALCOLM X

he wouldn't live to see the book published—and he was right.

I think my most indelible memory is of how ably he maintained his characteristic manner of controlled calm, when actually he lived amid a veritable cauldron of private and public pressures. Easily the source of most intense pressure was his role as the Nation of Islam's most public figure, while in fact he had been made virtually a pariah within the organization's top hierarchy. This status was due to, as Malcolm put it, "jealousies caused by others' refusal to accept that, when I did my appointed job as the Nation's spokesman, inevitably publicity would focus on me. I think Mr. Muhammad understood that, until others poisoned his mind against me." Nearly a year of our frequent interviewing had passed before he astonished me with a hint of that later public revelation.

Nonetheless, he carried on as "spokesman," maintaining such a grueling public-speaking schedule throughout the United States that some weeks he caught airplanes like taxis. And his blue Oldsmobile stayed on the go when he was in New York. There, particularly, he often faced hostile media people, and this helped him hone his verbal agility into practically an art form.

Malcolm was a master at deftly goading white verbal opponents into such a fury that they could only sputter almost incoherently. "The more the white man yelps, the more I know I have struck a nerve," Malcolm said. A hundred times, if once, I watched his face suddenly crease into a foxlike grin as an angry opponent struggled to retain composure, and then Malcolm would fire verbal missiles anew. He would turn a radio or television program to his advantage in a way he credited to the boxing ring's great Sugar Ray Robinson, who would dramatize a round's last thirty seconds. Similarly Malcolm would eye the big studio clock, and at the instant it showed thirty seconds to go, he'd pounce in and close the show with his own verbal barrage.

But there could also be quite another side of Malcolm X. I just have to laugh, recalling one night during our interviews when he was reminiscing about his finesse as a dancer. Springing up suddenly, with one hand grabbing a radiator pipe to represent a girl, he wildly lindy-hopped for maybe a full minute before suddenly stopping. He sat down, clearly embarrassed, and was practically surly for the rest of that session.

And I remember Malcolm one time laughing so raucously that he could hardly tell me the details of how he had once been menaced in his prison cell by an armed guard and how he had struck instant terror into the man. Abruptly jerking him so close that their noses touched, Malcolm had hissed, "You put a finger on me, I'll start a rumor you're really black, just passing for white!"

"I must be purer than Caesar's wife," Malcolm would often say, hypersensitive that any hint of wrongdoing could so easily become gossip capable of damaging his public image and credibility. And that public presence was indeed so awesome that wherever Malcolm appeared, it was rather like witnessing a force in motion. I saw the man's impact on people many different times and ways. On one afternoon when we were driving in Harlem, Malcolm suddenly jammed on the brakes and sprang from the car. Running across the street, to the sidewalk, Malcolm crouched like an avenger over three young black men whom he'd seen shooting dice near the entrance to the Schomburg Collection of Negro Literature and History, as it was then called. "Beyond those doors is the world's greatest collection of books about black people!" he raged at the young gamblers. "Other people are in there studying your people while you're outside shooting craps!" The three practically slinked away before Malcolm's wrath. He used to exclaim, "Man, lots of times I just wish I could start back in school, from about the sixth grade. Man, I'd be the last one out of that library every night!"

Although Malcolm X was acutely aware of the physical risks he steadily faced, he was determined not to let the danger muzzle his voice or inhibit his activities. He felt that his greatest safety lay in really trusting

'Malcolm was a genuine revolutionary, a virile impulse long since fled from the American way of life — in himself, indeed, he was a kind of revolution.'

—JAMES BALDWIN

'Malcolm was our manhood, our living...we will know him for what he was: a Prince— our own black shining Prince!— who didn't hesitate to die, because he loved us so.'

— OSSIE DAVIS

only a few people—and those few only to certain degrees. The late author Louis Lomax and I used to laugh about how we didn't discover until much later that once Malcolm had visited and given each of us interviews in different rooms in the same hotel, with never a mention to either about the other, although he knew well that Lomax and I were good friends. When Malcolm and I began the book project, he told me candidly, "I want you to know I trust you twenty-five percent." (Much later I felt great personal gratification when he upped the trust to seventy percent.) Now or then during our interviews he'd mention some people who seemed to me quite close to him—adding a startlingly low trust percentage.

Squarely atop Malcolm's trust list was his wife, Betty Shabazz, of whom he said, "She's the only person I'd trust with my life. That means I trust her more than I do myself." He felt genuine admiration for her, even awe, along with a deep sense of guilt that, while he was so often away from home, she somehow managed to be simultaneously a homemaker, a mother of three—then four—little girls, as well as his busy secretary and telephone answering service. He made it practically a fetish never to stop without immediately telephoning his Betty, saying candidly, "If my work won't let me be there, at least she can always know where I am."

I'm fascinated by the similarities between Malcolm X and Dr. Martin Luther King, Jr., that I observed. For instance, neither could have been much less concerned about acquiring material possessions, and both were obsessed with their work but felt guilty about being away from their families.

Vividly I remember Dr. King recalling among his hardest moments the feeling of mingled anger and shame he had when he and Mrs. King had to explain to their small daughter, Yolanda, that a radio ad for an event she wanted to attend was not meant for their race. Equally vividly I remember Malcolm's sadness one night when he had overlooked buying a present for his daughter, Attallah, for her fourth birthday—and how he beamed when

I surprised him with my intended gift, a black walking doll, and insisted that it be his gift instead.

The two men, who pursued their widely variant philosophies (toward the same goal, I believe), met only once, briefly, with photographers recording their smiles and handshakes during the 1963 March on Washington—and I smile, remembering the keen private concern each had for the other's opinion of him. I was in the midst of interviewing Malcolm for the book while I traveled to Atlanta to interview Dr. King for *Playboy* magazine. His ever pressured schedule meant I had to make several visits. Dr. King would always let maybe an hour pass before he'd casually ask, "By the way, what's Brother Malcolm saying about me these days?" I'd give some discreetly vague response, and then back in New York, I'd hear from Malcolm, "All right, tell me what he said about me!" to which I'd also give a vague reply. I'm convinced that privately the two men felt mutual admiration and respect. And I've surely no question that they would be pleased to know that their daughters, Yolanda and Attallah, today are friends who work closely together in a theater group. . . .

Malcolm X started me writing books, for which I am most grateful, and from the early days of working with him, I have tried to approach his degree of self-discipline. Looking back, I feel that Malcolm eminently succeeded in achieving a private goal that he once expressed to me: he believed that somehow, every day, he must demonstrate that only a defiant courage could break the fetters still impeding his beloved black people.

'Nobody can give you freedom. Nobody can give you equality or justice or anything. If you're a man, you take it.'

— MALCOLM X

eva peron

by V.S. Naipaul

OUTLINE IT LIKE A STORY BY BORGES.

The dictator is overthrown and more than half the people rejoice. The dictator had filled the jails and emptied the treasury. Like many dictators, he hadn't begun badly. He had wanted to make his country great. But he wasn't himself a great man; and perhaps the country couldn't be made great. Seventeen years pass. The country is still without great men; the treasury is still empty; and the people are on the verge of despair. They begin to remember that the dictator had a vision of the country's greatness, and that he was a strong man; they begin to remember that he had given much to the poor. The dictator is in exile. The people begin to agitate for his return. The dictator is now very old. But the people also remember the dictator's wife. She loved the poor and hated the rich, and she was young and beau-

---

Eva Perón, whose life was immortalized on stage and screen by the musical, <u>Evita</u>, was born in Los Toldos, Argentina. She was a radio and screen actress before her marriage to Argentinian President Juan Perón in 1945. Using her underprivileged background to identify with the poor in Argentina, she became a popular figure known for her lavish generosity, but also for her lavish lifestyle. Her body was embalmed upon her death in 1952, but kept hidden in Europe until 1976.

tiful. So she has remained, because she died young, in the middle of the dictatorship. And, miraculously, her body has not decomposed.

"That," Borges said, "is a story I could *never* write."

But at seventy-six, and after seventeen years of proscription and exile, Juan Perón, from the Madrid suburb known as the Iron Gate, dictates peace terms to the military regime in Argentina. In 1943, as an army colonel preaching a fierce nationalism, Perón became a power in Argentina; and from 1946 to 1955, through two election victories, he ruled as dictator. His wife Eva held no official position, but she ruled with Perón until 1952. In that year she died. She was expensively embalmed, and now her corpse is with Perón at the Iron Gate. . . .

And they have a saint: Eva Perón. "I remember I was very sad for many days," she wrote in 1952 in *La Razón de Mi Vida* (*My Life's Cause*), "when I discovered that in the world there were poor people and rich people; and the strange thing is that the existence of the poor didn't cause me as much pain as the knowledge that at the same time there were people who were rich." It was the basis of her political action. She preached a simple hate and a simple love. Hate for the rich: "Shall we burn down the Barrio Norte?" she would say to the crowds. "Shall I give you fire?" And love for "the common people," *el pueblo*; she used that word again and again and made it part of the Peronist vocabulary. She levied tribute from everyone for her Eva Perón Foundation; and she sat until three or four or five in the morning in the Ministry of Labor, giving away foundation money to supplicants, dispensing a personal justice. This was her "work": a child's vision of power, justice, and revenge.

She died in 1952, when she was thirty-three. And now in Argentina, after the proscribed years, the attempt to extirpate her name, she is a presence again. Her pictures are everywhere, touched up, seldom sharp, and often they seem deliberately garish, like religious pictures meant for the

---

'I watched for many years how a few rich families held Argentina's wealth and power in their hands. Peron brought in an eight-hour working day and fair wages to give poor workers a fair go.'

—EVA PERÓN

poor: a young woman of great beauty, with blond hair, a very white skin and the very red lips of the 1940s.

She was of the people and of the land. She was born in 1919 in Los Toldos, the dreariest of pampa small towns, built on the site of an Indian encampment, 150 flat miles west of Buenos Aires. The town gives an impression of flatness, of total exposure below the high sky. The dusty brick houses, red or white, are low, flat-fronted and flat-roofed, with an occasional balustrade; the paraíso trees have whitewashed trunks and are severely pollarded; the wide streets, away from the center, are still of dirt.

She was illegitimate; she was poor; and she lived for the first ten years of her life in a one-room house, which still stands. When she was fifteen she went to Buenos Aires to become an actress. Her speech was bad; she had a country girl's taste in clothes; her breasts were very small, her calves were heavy, and her ankles thickish. But within three months she had got her first job. And thereafter she charmed her way up. When she was twenty-five she met Perón; the following year they married.

Her commonness, her beauty, her success: they contribute to her sainthood. And her sexiness. "*Todos me acosan sexualmente*," she once said with irritation, in her actress days. "Everybody makes a pass at me." She was the macho's ideal victim-woman—don't those red lips still speak to the Argentine macho of her reputed skill in fellatio? But very soon she was beyond sex, and pure again. At twenty-nine she was dying from cancer of the uterus and hemorrhaging through the vagina; and her plumpish body began to waste away. Toward the end she weighed eighty pounds. One day she looked at some old official photographs of herself and began to cry. Another day she saw herself in a long mirror and said, "When I think of the trouble I went to to keep my legs slim! *Ahora que me veo estas piernitas me asusto.* Now it frightens me to look at these matchsticks."

But politically she never weakened. The Peronist revolution was

'Eva Perón wielded a power—spiritual and practical—that has few parallels outside of hereditary monarchy.'

—NICHOLAS FRASER

'Eva became a genuine populist heroine.... With a beautician's help and a hairdresser's skill, Evita was a golden fairy godmother to a yearning Argentina.'

—RICHARD RODRIGUEZ

going bad. Argentina's accumulated wartime wealth was running low; the colonial economy, unregenerated, plundered, mismanaged, was beginning to founder; the peso was falling; the workers, to whom so much had been given, were not always loyal. But she still cherished her especial pain that "there were people who were rich." Close to death, she told a gathering of provincial governors, "We mustn't pay too much attention to people who talk to us of prudence. We must be fanatical." The army was growing restive. She was willing to take them on. She wanted to arm the trade unions; and she did buy, through Prince Bernhard of the Netherlands, 5000 automatic pistols and 1500 machine guns, which, when they arrived, Perón, more prudent, gave to the police.

And all the time her private tragedy was being turned into the public passion play of the dictatorship. For her, who had turned Peronism into a religion, sainthood had long been decreed; and there is a story that for fifteen days before her death the man who was to embalm her was with her, to ensure that nothing was done that might damage the body. As soon as she died the embalming contract was signed. Was it for $100,000 or $300,000? The reports are confused. Dr. Ara, the Spanish embalmer—"a master," Perón called him—had first to make the body ready for a fifteen-day lying in state. The actual embalming took six months. The process remains secret. Dr. Ara, according to a Buenos Aires newspaper, has devoted two chapters of his memoirs (which are to be published only after his death) to the embalming of Eva Perón; color pictures of the corpse are also promised. Reports suggest that the blood was first replaced by alcohol, and then by heated glycerin (Perón himself says "paraffin and other special matter"), which was pumped in through the heel and an ear.

"I went three times to look at Evita," Perón wrote in 1956, after his overthrew, and when the embalmed body had disappeared. "The doors . . . were like the gates of eternity." He had the impression that she was only sleeping. The first time he went he wanted to touch her, but he feared that at the touch of his warm hand the body would turn to dust. Ara said, "Don't worry. She's as whole [*intacta*] now as when she was alive."

And now, twenty years later, her embalmed wasted body, once lost, now found, and no bigger, they say, than that of a twelve-year-old girl, only the blond hair as rich as in the time of health, waits with Perón at the Iron Gate.

Camelero, chanta: These are everyday Argentine words. A *camelero* is a line-shooter, a man who really has nothing to sell. The man who promised to take me to an estancia, and in his private airplane, was only doing *camelo*. The *chanta* is the man who will sell everything, the man without principles, the hollow man. Almost everybody, from the president down, is dismissed by somebody as a *chanta*.

The other word that recurs is *mediocre*. Argentines detest the mediocre and fear to be thought mediocre. It was one of Eva Perón's words of abuse. For her the Argentine aristocracy was always mediocre. And she was right. In a few years she shattered the myth of Argentina as an aristocratic colonial land. And no other myth, no other idea of the land, has been found to take its place.

'Without fanaticism, one can accomplish nothing.'

—EVA PERON

sitting bull

by Geoffrey C. Ward

N THE AUTUMN OF 1884 A YOUNG LAKOTA named Standing Bear, a student at the Carlisle Indian School, was granted permission to travel into Philadelphia and attend a stage show. Something called the "Sitting Bull Combination" was appearing there, a troupe that included the chief and holy man Sitting Bull and a handful of warriors—Spotted-Horn-bull, Gray Eagle, Flying By, Long Dog, Crow Eagle, along with several of their wives.

The performance consisted of a sort of tableau, in which the men sat smoking their pipes in front of a tepee and the women bent over a pot, pretending to cook a meal, while a white lecturer explained the "inner life of the Indian." Then, Sitting Bull, who neither spoke nor understood English, stepped forward and delivered an address in Lakota, explaining that the time for war against the whites had ended,

Sitting Bull was born into the Hunkpapa Sioux Nation in South Dakota in 1831. A warrior and medicine man, he was appointed principal Chief of the Sioux nation around 1867. After gold was discovered in the Black Hills on the reservation, Chief Sitting Bull joined with the Cheyenne and Arapaho to defeat General Custer's army. He was killed in a shootout with police in 1890.

'Now that we are poor, we are free. No white man controls our footsteps. If we must die, we die defending our rights.'

—SITTING BULL

that what was needed now was education for the children of his tribe.

A white translator stood at his side, allegedly rendering his remarks into English. But, Standing Bear noted, Sitting Bull's words and those of the white man actually bore no relation to one another. As the Lakota continued to speak of peace, his interpreter had him recounting in flamboyant detail just how his warriors had destroyed Custer's command at Little Bighorn. "He told so many lies," Standing Bear noted, "that I had to smile."

The showman was deliberately lying. Over the years white interpreters have more often simply gotten things wrong, usually exaggerating the supposed savagery of Native American culture in order to make those who nearly succeeded in destroying it seem more heroic, but sometimes conversely attributing to it a uniform austere nobility that was at best inaccurate and at worst patronizing. The simple proposition that Indians, like the whites whose intrusions they sought to withstand, were human beings who combined vices with virtues, strengths with weaknesses, still infuses too little historical writing about them.

Perhaps the most celebrated of all Indian leaders, Sitting Bull still emerges as a great Lakota patriot—a defensive shield as well as an offensive lance to his people—but he is also seen as a flawed statesman whose brave defiance may in the end have only made things worse.

Sitting Bull's life began about 1831 on the Grand River, at a place his people called Many Caches because of the food-storage pits they had dug there, and one is struck all through Utley's account [*The Lance and the Shield*] by the central role access to food in the form of buffalo played in the final years of Lakota freedom. Sitting Bull counted his first coup at fourteen, during a raid on the hunting grounds of the Lakotas' traditional enemies, the Crows. And it was in large part the damage whites did to the buffalo herds and the grass on which they fed that made him determined to drive them from his people's land.

It was both a tribute to Sitting Bull's own distinctive blend of bravery, wisdom, and spiritual power and evidence of his people's desperation in the face of destruction of the herds without which they could not imagine living, that in 1868 he was given a post that had never existed before in their world: "chief soldier," or head war chief, empowered to make decisions of war and peace for all the Lakotas. Sitting Bull was a profound conservative, determined never to abandon the old ways: "Look at me," he once shouted at a group of Assiniboins who had made their peace with the whites. "See if I am poor, or my people either. The whites may get me at last, as you say, but I will have good times till then. You are fools to make yourselves slaves to a piece of fat bacon, some hard-tack, and a little sugar and coffee." But he fought as a political revolutionary, principal chief of a people unaccustomed to following any leader.

The Lakota attachment to the Black Hills, which eventually led to the Custer fight, was partly spiritual—they held mountains to be uniquely sacred to them, though they had only relatively recently wrested them from other tribes—and partly practical: the slopes and valleys were alive with small game and ideally suited for winter camp. Sitting Bull called them a "food pack," by which, one Lakota explained, he meant that "Indians would rove around, but when they were in need of something, they could just go in and get it."

After the Little Bighorn, when Sitting Bull led his people north to escape the vengeful soldiers sent after him, he hoped to find permanent sanctuary in Canada, the land of the Grandmother, Queen Victoria. "I will remain what I am until I die," he said, "a hunter. And when there are no buffalo or other game, I will send my children to hunt and live on prairie mice, for where an Indian is shut up in one place his body becomes weak." But, again, scarcity of food forced him to shift his tactics. By 1880 very few buffalo appeared on the Canadian plains, thanks mostly to the hide hunters of Montana, and

'In one fight, Sitting Bull astonished everyone. He sat down in a meadow, in range of riflemen, casually filled a pipe, lit it, and smoked it, while bullets cut the grass around him.'

—LARRY MCMURTRY

'The great hope and purpose of his life was to unify the tribes, and hold the remaining lands of his people as a sacred inheritance for their children.'

—CATHERINE WELDON

when the Canadian government refused to accept responsibility for feeding Sitting Bull's starving people, he had little choice but to return to the United States and surrender. He composed a song to express his feelings: "A warrior/I have been/Now/It is all over/A hard time/I have."

His hard time continued. He was not implacably opposed to every government policy. He saw the need for schools, for example, and even learned to farm so well that he was put in charge of all the farmers in his neighborhood. But a tour with Buffalo Bill's Wild West show had convinced him of the error of alien ways: "The farther my people keep away from whites," he told a woman missionary, "the better I shall be satisfied. The white people are wicked, and I don't want my woman to become as the white women I have seen have lived. I want you to teach my people to read and write, but they must not become white people in their ways; it is too bad a life, I could not let them do it." He saw no need to convert to Christianity, resisted attempts further to reduce the reservation whose border he already found confining, and led the opposition to the Dawes Severalty Act, which divided tribal lands into individual allotments.

When the Ghost Dance agitation began in 1889, promising a reborn Indian world filled with buffalo and free of whites, he was a skeptic. But when he agreed to travel to the Pine Ridge Agency and look into it further, the Indian agent, terrified that he might urge that arms be taken up again, sent Indian police to arrest him. In the shoot-out that followed, on December 15, 1890, Sitting Bull, seven of his followers, and six policemen were all killed in and around his cabin that stood just across Great River from Many Caches, the spot where he had been born fifty-nine years before.

Shortly after he surrendered and six years before his death, Sitting Bull told a newspaperman of his doubts about the future: "White men like to dig in the ground for their food. My people prefer to hunt the buffalo as their fathers did. . . . The life my people want is a life of freedom. I have seen nothing that a white man has, houses or railways or clothing or food, that is as good as the right to move in the open country and live in our own fashion."

'My friends and relatives, let us stand as one family, as we did before the white people led us astray.'

—SITTING BULL

the dalai lama

by Pico Iyer

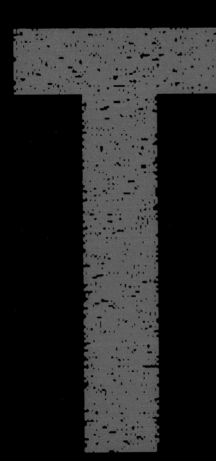

T HE DALAI LAMA IS ONE FOR WHICH I CAN think of no precedent or parallel. Trained for 18 years in the intricacies of Tibetan Buddhist metaphysics, one of the most accomplished philosophers in his tradition has spent most of the past half-century entangled in geopolitics, trying to protect and rescue his homeland from the Chinese forces that attacked in 1950 and drove him into exile nine years later. His cause is not made easier by the facts that much of the world is trying to court China, the world's largest marketplace, and that he is the guest of a huge nation with problems of its own that would rather he kept quiet. And, as church and state incarnate, the Dalai Lama, winner of the 1989 Nobel Prize for Peace, finds himself denied the privileges of a full-fledged political leader even as he cannot enjoy the peaceful immunity of a purely religious figure.

The Dalai Lama, born into a peasant family in Takster, China, in 1935, was designated the 14th Dalai Lama in 1937 and then forced into exile by the Chinese government in 1959. He won the Nobel Peace Prize in 1989 for his continued and committed efforts to liberate Tibet in a nonviolent manner.

The ever pragmatic Tibetan has responded to this predicament by taking his cause directly to the world, traveling almost constantly (on a refugee's yellow "identity certificate"), answering questions in 20,000-seat pop-concert halls about everything from Jack Kevorkian to TV violence, and letting his speeches be broadcast live on the floor of London dance clubs. This has led to the unlikely sight of a "simple monk" (as he always calls himself)—born and raised in a culture that had scarcely seen a Westerner when the century began—now seeming as visible, and even as fashionable, a figure as Richard Gere. John Cleese speaks out for him in London, Henri Cartier-Bresson records his teachings around France, Adam Yauch of the Beastie Boys interviews him in Rome for *Rolling Stone.* In the past few years he has opened 11 Offices of Tibet, everywhere from Canberra to Moscow, and last year alone provided prefaces and forewords for roughly 30 books. The 14th Dalai Lama is surely the only Ocean of Wisdom, Holder of the White Lotus and Protector of the Land of Snows to serve as guest editor of French *Vogue.*

To appreciate fully the incongruities of Tenzin Gyatso's life in the celebrity age, you have to recall that he was born in a cow-shed in a tiny farming village in what was locally known as the Wood Hog Year (1935). The previous Dalai Lama, the 13th, had been one of the great reforming spirits of a tradition whose leaders had all too often been ineffectual boys manipulated by regents. Beset by imperialists of all stripes, the farsighted Lama, in his last written testament, predicted a time in Tibet's history, soon, when "monks and monasteries will be destroyed . . . [and] all beings will be sunk in great hardship and overwhelming fear."

Upon his death, the senior monks of Lhasa set about finding his successor in the traditional fashion. The regent went to the sacred lake of Lhamoi Lhatso, famous for its visions, and saw in its waters an image of a gold-roofed, three-story monastery beside a winding path. Other signs

'It is not enough, as communist systems have assumed, merely to provide people with food, shelter and clothing. The deeper human nature needs to breathe the precious air of liberty.'

—THE DALAI LAMA

appeared. The embalmed body of the departed ruler seemed to move from pointing south to pointing toward the northeast. And auspicious cloud formations also appeared in the northeast. When a search party of monks arrived at the 20-family settlement of Takster, in the northeastern province of Amdo, its members were startled to find a gold-roofed, three-story monastery beside a winding path. They were even more taken aback when a two-year-old boy greeted them with familiarity and addressed their leader, disguised as a servant, by the name of his temple in distant Lhasa. The mischievous toddler, who slept in the kitchen of a mud-and-stone house, would become the 14th Dalai Lama.

At the age of four he was installed upon the Lion Throne in Lhasa and inducted into a formidable course of monastic studies. By the age of six he was choosing his own regent, and by the time he was 11 he was weathering civil uprising. The Dalai Lama has written with typical warmth about his unworldly boyhood in the cold, dark, thousand-room Potala Palace, playing games with the palace sweepers, rigging up a hand-cranked projector on which he could watch Tarzan movies and *Henry V*, and clobbering his only real playmate—his immediate elder brother Lobsang Samten—serene in the knowledge that no one would readily punish a boy regarded as the incarnation of the god of compassion. Yet the dominant characteristic of his childhood was its loneliness. Often, he recalls, he would go onto the rooftop of his palace and watch the other boys of Lhasa playing in the streets. And each time his brother left, he remembers "standing at the window, watching, my heart full of sorrow as he disappeared into the distance."

Tibet itself (with an army of just 8,500) was in an equally vulnerable state of remoteness when Chinese forces, newly united by Mao Zedong, attacked its eastern frontiers in 1950. Hurriedly, on the advice of the State Oracle (who delivered counsel while in a trance), the 15-year-old boy was invested with full political authority, and while still in his teens, he

'It is easier to revere or dismiss him than to treat him seriously, because to do so means getting into disturbing questions of...whether we are open to ethical and political transformation.'

—LYNN ROSELLIN

traveled to Beijing in 1954, against the wishes of his protective people, to negotiate face to face with Mao.

Five years later, when angry Tibetans rose up ever more fiercely against Chinese aggression, their young leader consulted the State Oracle again and, one night, dressed as a humble soldier, slipped out of his summer palace, with his family and some bodyguards. For two weeks the party traveled over the highest mountains on earth, dodging Chinese planes and moving only under the cover of darkness, until at last, suffering from dysentery and on the back of a hybrid yak, the Dalai Lama arrived in India and began a new life in exile. . . .

When I left Dharamsala at dawn, the Dalai Lama was leading his monks in a three-hour ceremony while the sun came up behind the distant snowcaps. It struck me that the man has lived out a kind of archetypal destiny of our times: a boy born in a peasant village in a world that had scarcely seen a wheel has ended up confronting the great forces of the day—exile, global travel and, especially, the mass media; and a man from a culture known as the "Forbidden Kingdom" now faces machine guns on the one hand and Chinese discos around the Potala Palace on the other. While Tibet is eroded in its homeland, it threatens to be commodified—or turned into an exotic accessory—abroad.

Yet to this state-of-the-art challenge the Dalai Lama brings, in his own words, a "radical informality," a gift for cutting through to the heart of things and an unusually open and practical mind. If I had to single out one sovereign quality in him, it would be alertness, whether he's reminding me of a sentence he delivered to me seven years before or picking out a friend's face in the middle of a jam-packed prayer hall.

This mindfulness, as Buddhists might call it, is particularly critical these days as the Dalai Lama finds himself more and more appealing to people who know nothing of his philosophy—and may even be hostile to it.

'The Dalai Lama has developed his philosophy of peace from a great reverence for all things living and upon the concept of universal responsibility embracing all mankind as well as nature.'

—THE NOBEL PRIZE COMMITTEE

The Tibetan has delivered lectures on the Gospels, celebrated the Internet as a talisman of human interdependence and, especially, mastered the art of talking to ordinary people in ordinary human terms, about "spirituality without faith." As his longtime friend the composer Philip Glass says, "He talks about compassion, he talks about right living. And it's very powerful and persuasive to people because it's clear he's not there to convert them."

The Dalai Lama is unbending on this point. "Out of 5.8 million people in the world," he tells me, "the majority of them are certainly not believers. We can't argue with them, tell them they should be believers. No! Impossible! And, realistically speaking, if the majority of humanity remains nonbelievers, it doesn't matter. No problem! The problem is that the majority have lost, or ignore, the deeper human values—compassion, a sense of responsibility. That is our big concern. For whenever there is a community without deeper human values, then even one single family cannot be a happy family." For, if we merely want to be happy, he says—though he has been forced from his homeland, seen 1.2 million of his people killed and had nearly all his 6,000 monasteries destroyed—it pays to be kind. Kindness, he says over and over, only stands to reason.

'Brute force, no matter how strongly applied, can never subdue the basic human desire for freedom and dignity.'

—THE DALAI LAMA

by Anna Husarska

EING ARRESTED IS NEVER PLEASANT, BUT, when your detainers are wearing flip-flops and sarongs, it's somehow less threatening. I had already given my exposed rolls of film to an acquaintance to smuggle to Burma, so the police had to settle for an unexposed one left in the camera. My notes, in Polish, were briefly examined, then ignored. And with that I was summarily deported—just a few hours before my planned departure.

I had been taken into custody just after leaving the headquarters of the opposition National League for Democracy (NLD) in Rangoon, where I had met with 1991 Nobel Peace Prize winner Aung San Suu Kyi. Throughout my stay in Burma, everyone kept asking me excitedly, "Will you see the Lady?" So it seemed natural that my interrogators, too, would ask the same thing.

Lady" is a testament to how she has become the absolute center of e

one's attention. In the junta mouthpiece *The New Light of Myanmar*,

"[w]hite alien's wife Suu Kyi who is conspiring to sell the Union int

hands of neocolonialists." The paper also runs poems about her. A sa

from the December 23, 1998 edition: "Here, woman, the people k

ing/The story of puppet on strings/Nothing good you are doing/

when not in power/Adorned with deception of yours/Gives ord

woman inferior/Just retrace your steps/To your husband, go back

were not asked to come."

To the Burmese people, however, Suu Kyi is practically a sair

repository of all their hopes—which is both uplifting and a little unset

There is a spontaneous cult of personality around her. A business w

asked me: "You like my dress top? *She* wears a similar one." A bike i

in Mandalay explained it to me according to a simple formula: "She

daughter of the father of the nation. So the Lady *is* the nation." To pro

he gave me five different banknotes emblazoned with the picture o

father, Gen. Aung San. Throughout Burma, streets, parks, and squar

named after him, and his statues are everywhere. Although he was as

nated in July 1947, six months before Burma's independence, he

national hero and, in a paradoxical twist, the founder of the Burmese A

Kyi had come to visit her ailing mother from Oxford, England, where she had been living with her British husband, Michael Aris, and their two sons. Even before they were married, she had written to Aris: "I only ask one thing, that, should my people need me, you would help me to do my duty by them."

In the wake of the crackdown, the Burmese people's need was all too apparent. On August 26, Suu Kyi spoke at a rally outside Rangoon's Shwedagon Pagoda: "I could not, as my father's daughter, remain indifferent to all that was going on. This national crisis could, in fact, be called the second struggle for national independence." This speech sealed her position as the leader of the burgeoning democratic movement.

By September, the death toll was in the thousands. The generals formed the State Law and Order Restoration Council, known as SLORC—a rather unfortunate name that, on the advice of a Washington-based public relations firm, was later changed to SPDC for State Peace and Development Council. Within a week of SLORC's formation, Suu Kyi and dissident Burmese officers founded the NLD. In 1990, demonstrating its total ignorance of the national mood, the junta confidently organized elections. The NLD, led by Suu Kyi, won 82 percent of the seats even though, a few months earlier, the generals had put her under house arrest. The junta refused to hand over power and increased repression.

Ne Win, now 88, continues to wield power from behind the scenes. As for Suu Kyi, she remained under house arrest for the next six years. Nowadays, it is almost impossible to see her. Her family house is off-limits for most locals and foreigners; even DHL can't deliver packages. And her movements are restricted when she tries to visit supporters outside Rangoon. Twice last summer, when the military blocked her route, she conducted a silent protest by remaining in her car for several days. . . .

When I arrived, the hall downstairs was filled with women and their malnourished children, many crying. Suu Kyi stood at the front,

'Anything that creates understanding in the long run makes for less violence.'

—AUNG SAN SUU KYI

'I had been moved by Martin Luther King's "I Have a Dream" speech and how he tried to better the lot of black people without fostering hate. It's hate that is the problem, not violence.'

—AUNG SAN SUU KYI

handing out spoonfuls of some type of formula to each child as his name was called on a bullhorn. Each mother received a bottle of the formula to take home. This long, noisy, exhausting event was obviously a way for her to stay in touch with her people, just like the distribution of rice that she does personally every Monday. However, attendance is low because of intimidation by military intelligence.

Finally, Suu Kyi joined us. At age 53, she looks a good 20 years younger. She is graceful and possesses what the French call *charme hypnotique*, yet she is also tough and matter-of-fact. At the time, I did not know the news that she knew and was probably devastated by: namely, that her husband, whom she had not seen since Christmas of 1995, was dying of prostate cancer. The authorities have refused to grant him a visa, and thus Suu Kyi has been given a Hobson's choice. If she leaves Burma to see her husband, she will almost certainly not be allowed back in. And, if she stays, she will never get a chance to say goodbye to Aris before he dies.

I asked her about a rumored deal whereby, in exchange for World Bank aid and a promise by the NLD to rescind its calls to convene the parliament, the generals would release political prisoners, open a dialogue with the NLD, and allow it to function as a political party. Suu Kyi pooh-poohed the rumor: the NLD was ready to talk and have negotiations with the authorities with or without the World Bank. But the NLD would never put a price tag on giving up its democratic right to convene parliament.

Perhaps Suu Kyi wanted to discredit the deal because it would have interfered with current international economic sanctions, which, the NLD maintains, are vital. But, as one Western diplomat pointed out to me, Burma's very backwardness—the only major foreign investment here is a controversial pipeline in the south owned jointly by Total of France, Unocal of the United States, and the Petroleum Authority of Thailand (with 15 percent staying in the hands of the Burmese junta)—makes the country less vulnerable to economic pressure. "Can a country that for years was closed to the outside world and practiced autarky be seriously hit by isolation?" the diplomat asked.

I asked Suu Kyi whether she did not fear that the Burmese, seeing no positive results from her pacifist resistance methods, would turn to violence like the Albanians in Kosovo have. She snapped that the Burmese knew hers was the right way—Southeast Asia is not the Balkans. Suu Kyi was very impressed by Vaclav Havel's classic essay "*The Power of the Powerless.*" We spoke about Havel's house arrest, and this led to a discussion of the different ways totalitarian regimes treat dissidents. I asked if the authorities' campaign against the NLD was effective. "Yes," said Suu Kyi. "This is very serious; imprisonments are seriously hampering our work."

Nonetheless, a Western diplomat who has been in Rangoon for a long time called the whole Burmese political scene "virtual politics": the SPDC has no credibility while the NLD is bottled up. Although the NLD recently created shadow ministries, there is not much it can do with half of the members of parliament "guest-housed." "What will be left?" the diplomat asked with genuine worry. "Just a core of heroes around the Lady?"

In Mandalay, an 84-year-old woman asked me, "Do you think I will *live* to see this change?" It took all my optimism to grumble that maybe the dissidents can turn the tables on Gen. Ne Win and make the number nine work for them—i.e., overthrow the junta on 9/9/99. But she knew I said it out of sympathy for her rather than conviction. But perhaps not everything is lost. The policewoman who searched me after my arrest was assigned to watch me at the airport on the last leg of my deportation. Boredom made her talkative. It turned out that she had not been told why she was searching me. "What did you do to get into trouble?" she asked. "You don't know? I went to see Aung San Suu Kyi," I said. "Oh, you saw the Lady!" she exclaimed. "How is she?"

'Like Nelson Mandela before her, Aung San Suu Kyi has come to be seen as a symbol of heroic and peaceful resistance in the face of oppression.'

—ARLENE GREGORIUS

aleksandr solzhenitsyn

by Nina Khrushcheva

THE NOTION THAT ALEKSANDR SOLZHENITSYN is the most tragic figure of twentieth-century Russia has become a cliché. A man ennobled by suffering, whose courage and unique experience made him "a moral compass for the nation," has been consumed by that same suffering. At the age of 80, Aleksandr Isaevich has become a living shell for his former artistic and political splendor. For a writer with real gifts, such a fate is tragic indeed.

In Russia, once you are "god" (a martyr, a czar, a president), you remain so forever. To step away from the spotlight in your lifetime, to recognize your limits, is something few Russians have been able to master. Ever since the publication of *One Day in the Life of Ivan Denisovich* in the early sixties, and more so after *The Gulag Archipelago* appeared in the West a decade later,

Alexander Isaevich Solzhenitsyn was born in Kislovodsk, Russia, in 1918. He fought in World War II, and was imprisoned for unfavorable comment on Stalin's conduct of the war. On his release, he became a teacher and started to write. His first novel, <u>One Day in the Life of Ivan Denisovich</u> (1962), set in a prison camp, was acclaimed both in the USSR and the West. He was expelled from the Soviet Writers' Union in 1969 and awarded the Nobel Prize for Literature. His later books include <u>The Gulag Archipelago</u>, an account of the Stalinist terror, for which he was arrested and exiled (1974).

'He doesn't deserve having anyone argue with him. Our Soviet reality exposes him as an untalented scribbler.'

—FROM PRAVDA, THE SOVIET NEWSPAPER

Solzhenitsyn has stood as the most monumental, respected, even revered figure in contemporary Russian culture. The injustice of his being unable to receive his Nobel Prize in Literature in person (it was awarded in 1970) and his final expulsion from his homeland in 1974 made him also a historical figure of global importance.

After two years in Europe he moved to the United States, where the snows and birches of Vermont reminded the exiled writer of his native Russia. So great was the author's desire to preserve his Russianness that he surrounded himself with a tall fence and refused to deal with America and the world altogether. The great icon of Russia's *samizdat* dissident movement, aware of this powerful responsibility to remain "great," was afraid to corrupt and Westernize his unique and mysterious Russian soul. This vanity and contempt for the outside world was revenged by fate—*The Red Wheel*, a four-part fictional work, which Solzhenitsyn spent almost all his exile writing, is sadly little more than a crank's mausoleum within which his Nobel Prize-worthy talent has been interred.

Solzhenitsyn's great gift was in witness. His best works are essentially autobiographical. *The First Circle* (which was circulated in clandestine form in 1966) came out of the author's experience as a mathematician in a group attached to the scientific research institute of the secret police during his early postwar imprisonment. The gulag camp for political prisoners in which he found himself some years later became the setting for *One Day in the Life of Ivan Denisovich* (published in the literary journal *Novy Mir* in 1962). In internal exile in Tashkent he was stricken with stomach cancer; having survived radiation treatments, he employed the hospital as setting for *Cancer Ward* (circulated clandestinely in 1966). Finally, monumentally, in 1973 *The Gulag Archipelago* appeared, topping them all with its great artistic truth. In

Solzhenitsyn's own words, "In this book there are no fictitious persons, nor fictitious events," but the result nonetheless was infinitely powerful literature.

When in the early seventies the still-unpublished *Gulag* secretly circulated in Moscow, the retired Nikita Khrushchev, who had vigorously supported the first publication of *Ivan Denisovich* while still in power, read the manuscript. Khrushchev was pleased to see the righteousness of his political battle for de-Stalinization confirmed by great art. However, his wife, Nina Petrovna, refused to finish the book after glancing through only a few chapters. Her reasoning was, "It cannot be true. If it were true we wouldn't be alive now." Even knowing many of Stalin's acts at first hand, she could not accept the artistic account of those crimes; such was the power of Solzhenitsyn's incredible talent.

But being a witness was not enough for him; the temptation to be a prophet was too overwhelming. At hand was a topic more important than his own life: Russia. And in 1971 the world witnessed the appearance of *August 1914*, the first part, or "Knot" (a historical turning point), of *The Red Wheel*, a story of how the wheel of history brought Russia to the Communist Revolution.

This attempt was great and promising. Although the novel was not easy to follow, its rough and uneven style was compensated for through its presentation of a dramatically new interpretation of Russian history. Inspired by the example of Jesus in the desert, Aleksandr Isaevich sacrificed worldliness for the cause: While isolating himself in Vermont, he began to convey great historical and fictional revelation of his country's misfortunes. But the artificial, hermetic environment of the mountains of New England produced an equally artificial pre-revolutionary Russia. When the long-awaited

'When comparisons of are made with Tolstoy, Dostoevsky and Turgenev, this is not hyperbole.'

—HARRISON SALISBURY

> **'The tasks of the writer cannot be reduced to defense or criticism of... government. The tasks of the writer are connected with the secrets of the human heart and conscience.'**
>
> **—ALEKSANDR SOLZHENITSYN**

four Knots of *The Red Wheel* were finally published in Russia in the nineties, one Moscow writer noted, "In our time you just can't live and write in a vacuum. He may be great, but for another time and another generation."

The writer majestically pontificates with little respect for the reader, regardless of one's attention, interest or the necessity of the narrative itself. His czarlike and prophetic utterances— "Art demands distillation of actuality"—and his referral to himself in the third-person as "the author" and "he" sound frighteningly above humanity. Jesus did go to the desert to acquire truth, but he was God, after all. Solzhenitsyn (because it was so harshly earned) had a better chance at prophecy than many others, but the sad truth is that humans rarely forgive pontification in other human beings.

When Aleksandr Isaevich returned to Russia in 1994 after twenty years of exile, he was greeted as a saint, a martyr, almost God himself. He was considered the hope of the people in general, as well as the new post-Communist regime. He was expected to enlighten, to lead, to explain. Yeltsin and Gorbachev, democrats and Communists, nationalists and socialists, met with him to learn from the great man's wisdom. His collected works came out, all his articles and essays were published. He was given any tribute he desired, was asked to anchor a TV and a radio show. Russia finally proved wrong the famous maxim that a prophet is not honored in his homeland. The country had its prophet back and respectfully clung to his every word. They waited for his words, either on TV screens or in books, with breathless eagerness.

Grave disappointment ensued. I don't know anyone who failed to switch to another channel when Solzhenitsyn was *veshchat* in his weekly programs, or was able to get through the writer's bookish and dead style. After a year or so both the TV and the radio show were canceled. Aleksandr Isaevich accused the media authorities of anti-patriotism and conspiracy, but, to tell the truth, his public appearances were boring, declaratory and uninformative. After *Ivan Denisovich*, *The Gulag Archipelago* and *Cancer Ward*, the great man had lot of words, but nothing to say.

'One word of truth shall outweigh the whole world.'

—ALEKSANDR SOLZHENITSYN

pancho villa

by Friedrich Katz

T WAS A SCENE HE WOULD HAVE LOVED. Despite the cold, blustery weather that November day in 1976, throngs of people lined the street in the old city of Parral in the state of Chihuahua. They had heard the news that Pancho Villa's remains, which were buried in Parral, would, as the result of a decree passed by the Mexican president, be transferred to the Monument of the Revolution in Mexico City. This constituted a belated recognition by a Mexican government of his revolutionary merits. As Villa's casket, flanked by members of his family, came into view, masses of people began clapping and cheering. Many burst into the old rallying cry of "Viva Villa!"

What would have impressed Villa was the fact that practically none of these enthusiastic spectators had ever known him, since more than 50 years had elapsed since his

Pancho Villa, born in Mexico in 1878, joined in Francisco Madero's revolution against Mexican dictator Porfirio Díaz. Villa served under General Victoriano Huerta until Huerta sentenced him to death for insubordination. Villa then fled to the United States. He returned to Mexico in 1913 to form La Division del Norte and joining Venustiano Carranza, successfully overthrew General Huerta's government. Villa and Carranza became enemies, and Villa continued his revolutionary movement against Carranza until Villa's retirement in 1920. He was assassinated in 1923.

'Pancho Villa, so the saying goes, was "hated by thousands and loved by millions." He was a Robin Hood to many and a cruel cold-blooded killer to others.'

—JORGE MEJÍA PRIETO

death, and even the parents of many who now stood on the streets of Parral to watch him go to join the remains of his enemies in the mausoleum of revolutionary heroes in Mexico City had never seen, heard, or met him. It was a measure of the influence he still exercised in his adopted state that so many years after his death, thousands came out to cheer him. Another expression of the emotions his memory aroused was the fact that thousands of others are said to have refused to come out, that many sent harsh letters of protest to the newspapers, and some avidly read Rodrigo Alonso Cortés's 1972 book *Francisco Villa, el quinto jinete del apocalipsis* (*Pancho Villa, the Fifth Rider of the Apocalypse*), which depicts Villa as a monster, and similar works.

These competing reactions reflect the contradictions of the man himself and the contradictions within the many legends about him.

There are three basic versions of Villa's early life, which I shall call the white legend, the black legend, and the epic legend. The first, based largely on Villa's own reminiscences, portrays him as a victim of the social and economic system of Porfirian Mexico: a man the authorities prevented from living a quiet, law-abiding life, although he attempted to do so.

"The tragedy of my life begins on September 22, 1894, when I was sixteen years old," Villa recounts in his memoirs.

When he returned home from work that day in 1894, he found Don Agustín López Negrete, "the Master, the owner of the lives and honor of us the poor people," standing in front of his mother, who was telling him: "Go away from my house! Why do you want to take my daughter?"

When he heard these words, the young Doroteo Arango [Villa's original name] became so furious that he ran to the house of his cousin Romualdo Franco, took the latter's gun, and shot López Negrete in the foot.

From that moment on, Doroteo led the life of an outlaw in the mountains of Durango, relentlessly pursued by the authorities. He became convinced that surviving alone was too difficult and so decided to join two outlaws who were roaming in the vicinity, Ignacio Parra and Refugio Alvarado. Before they accepted him into their company, the two men told him:

> "Look, young man, if you want to go with us, you have to do everything that we tell you. We know how to kill and rob. We tell you this so that you should not be afraid." These crude words, clear and precise like the blow of a hammer, did not intimidate me. . . . men who pompously call themselves honest also kill and rob. In the name of the law that they apply for the benefit and protection of the few in order to threaten and sacrifice the many, the high authorities of the people rob and kill with the greatest impunity.

A new and far more agreeable life now began for the newly named Francisco Villa. Instead of being a hunted fugitive, barely managing to survive, he became a successful outlaw, reaping the rewards of banditry.

The most systematic and comprehensive version of the black legend was written by Celia Herrera, a member of a family who developed a kind of blood feud with Villa, and many of whose members Villa killed.

Herrera depicts a vicious killer and murderer without any redeeming qualities. According to this account, Abraham González never asked Villa to participate in the revolution. In fact, he got involved only by coincidence: he was visiting a girlfriend at a small ranch when a federal force, believing that some revolutionaries were hidden there, attacked it. Thinking that they were pursuing him, Villa shot back and fled. He then decided to join Pascual Orozco, together with his gang. Orozco at first refused, since he considered Villa nothing more than a bandit. While negotiations were going on, federal troops attacked Orozco, Villa joined in responding to the attack, and Orozco reluctantly accepted the bandit into his army. He was to regret this decision, since Villa later stole the pay des-

'I understood for the first time that all the suffering, all the hatred, all the rebellions that had accumulated in my soul during so many years of fighting had given me such a strength of conviction that I could offer all to my country.'

—PANCHO VILLA

tined for the revolutionary troops.

No one has better described the epic legend than the U.S. correspondent John Reed:

> "An immense body of popular legend grew up among the peons around his name. There are many traditional songs and ballads, celebrating his exploits—you can hear the shepherds singing them around their fires at night, repeating verses handed down by their fathers or composing others extemporaneously. For instance, they tell the story of how Villa, fired by the story of the misery of the peons at the hacienda of Los Alamos, gathered a small army and descended upon the big house, which he looted and distributed the spoils among the poor people. He drove off thousands of cattle from the Terrazas range and ran them across the border. He would suddenly descend upon a prosperous mine and seize the bullion. When he needed corn he captured a granary belonging to a rich man. He recruited almost openly in the villages, far removed from the well traveled roads and railways, organizing the outlaws of the mountains."

There are legends of Villa the Robin Hood, Villa the Napoleon of Mexico, Villa the ruthless killer, Villa the womanizer, and Villa as the only foreigner who has attacked the mainland of the United States since the war of 1812 and gotten away with it. Whether correct or incorrect, exaggerated or true to life, these legends have resulted in Pancho Villa the leader obscuring his movement, and the myths obscuring the leader. So much attention has focused on Villa himself that the characteristics of his movement that in many respects make it unique in Latin America, and in some ways among twentieth-century revolutions, have either been forgotten or neglected. Villa's División del Norte was probably the largest revolutionary army that Latin America ever produced. The revolution he led was the

'Villa, fired by the misery of the peons at the hacienda of Los Alamos, gathered a small army and descended upon the big house, which he looted and distributed the spoils among the poor people.'

—JOHN REED

only social revolution ever to occur along the border of the United States. It was also one of the few genuine revolutions produced by what might best be described as a frontier region on the American continent.

Perhaps even more exceptional, this was one of the few revolutionary movements with which a U.S. administration in the twentieth century attempted, not only to come to terms, but even to forge an alliance. Equally remarkable, the Villa movement was part of one of the few twentieth-century revolutions that still enjoy enormous legitimacy in its own people's eyes. In Russia, Leningrad has been renamed St. Petersburg, and in China, students questioned Mao's revolution on Tiananmen Square, but no one in Mexico is thinking of renaming the streets that bear the names of Villa or of other revolutionary heroes. In fact, not only the official government party but one of the main opposition parties and a newly emerged guerrilla movement in Chiapas all claim to be the legitimate heirs of the revolutionaries of 1919—20, among whom Villa's movement constituted a decisive force.

Finally, both Villa and the leader of the strongest popular movement in southern Mexico, Emiliano Zapata, differed in significant ways from the revolutionary leaders that emerged elsewhere in the twentieth century. In contrast to such men as Lenin, Mao Tse-tung, Ho Chi Minh, or Fidel Castro, all of whom were highly educated intellectuals who led well-organized political movements, both Villa and Zapata came from the lower classes of society, had little education, and organized no political parties.

There is little doubt that new documents relating to and new interpretations of both Villa and his movement will emerge. In addition, as has been the case with Danton, Robespierre, and other major revolutionary figures (and Villa, whatever one may think of him, was a major revolutionary figure), each generation will look at Villa from a different perspective, so that discussions on this subject will continue for years to come.

'History is written by victors, but legends are written by the people. For that reason, the name of Francisco Villa has remained enshrined forever in the heart of the poor.'

—UNKNOWN SPEAKER AT VILLA'S FUNERAL

nelson mandela

by André Brink

S THE WORLD'S MOST FAMOUS PRISONER and, now, his country's leader, he exemplifies a moral integrity that shines far beyond South Africa.

In a recent television broadcast BBC commentator Brian Walden argued that Nelson Mandela, "perhaps the most generally admired figure of our age, falls short of the giants of the past." Mandela himself argues that "I was not a messiah, but an ordinary man who had become a leader because of extraordinary circumstances." Clearly, a changing world demands redefinition of old concepts.

In the revolution led by Mandela to transform a model of racial division and oppression into an open democracy, he demonstrated that he didn't flinch from taking up arms, but his real qualities came to the fore after his time as an activist—during his 27 years in prison and in the eight

Nelson Mandela was born in Transkei, South Africa, in 1918. He was a lawyer in Johannesburg before joining the African National Congress. Mandela received a life sentence for his political activities in 1964, though he continued his work against apartheid from prison until 1990, when President F.W. de Klerk lifted the ban on the African National Congress and Mandela was released. In 1993 he shared the Nobel Peace Prize with de Klerk, and then was elected president of South Africa in 1994.

years since his release, when he had to negotiate the challenge of turning a myth into a man.

Rolihlahla Mandela was born deep in the black homeland of Transkei on July 18, 1918. His first name could be interpreted, prophetically, as "troublemaker." The Nelson was added later, by a primary school teacher with delusions of imperial splendor. Mandela's boyhood was peaceful enough, spent on cattle herding and other rural pursuits, until the death of his father landed him in the care of a powerful relative, the acting regent of the Thembu people. But it was only after he left the missionary College of Fort Hare, where he had become involved in student protests against the white colonial rule of the institution, that he set out on the long walk toward personal and national liberation.

Having run away from his guardian to avoid an arranged marriage, he joined a law firm in Johannesburg as an apprentice. Years of daily exposure to the inhumanities of apartheid, where being black reduced one to the status of a nonperson, kindled in him a kind of absurd courage to change the world. It meant that instead of the easy life in a rural setting he'd been brought up for, or even a modest measure of success as a lawyer, his only future certainties would be sacrifice and suffering, with little hope of success in a country in which centuries of colonial rule had concentrated all political and military power, all access to education, and most of the wealth in the hands of the white minority. The classic conditions for a successful revolution were almost wholly absent: the great mass of have-nots had been humbled into docile collusion, the geographic expanse of the country hampered communication and mobility, and the prospects of a race war were not only unrealistic but also horrendous.

In these circumstances Mandela opted for nonviolence as a strategy. He joined the Youth League of the African National Congress and became involved in programs of passive resistance against the laws that forced

'We all see ourselves reflected in his glory. A glory that arises in his humility, his sense of forgiveness.'

—THABO MBEKI

blacks to carry passes and kept them in a position of permanent servility.

Exasperated, the government mounted a massive treason trial against its main opponents, Mandela among them. It dragged on for five years, until 1961, ending in the acquittal of all 156 accused. But by that time the country had been convulsed by the massacre of peaceful black demonstrators at Sharpeville in March 1960, and the government was intent on crushing all opposition. Most liberation movements, including the African National Congress (ANC), were banned. Earning a reputation as the Black Pimpernel, Mandela went underground for more than a year and traveled abroad to enlist support for the ANC.

Soon after his return, he was arrested and sentenced to imprisonment on Robben Island for five years; within months practically all the leaders of the ANC. were arrested. Mandela was hauled from prison to face with them an almost certain death sentence. His statement from the dock was destined to smolder in the homes and servant quarters, the shacks and shebeens and huts and hovels of the oppressed, and to burn in the conscience of the world: "During my lifetime I have dedicated myself to the struggle of the African people. I have fought against white domination, and I have fought against black domination. I have cherished the ideal of a democratic and free society in which all persons live together in harmony and with equal opportunities. It is an ideal which I hope to live for and to achieve. But, if needs be, it is an ideal for which I am prepared to die."

Without any attempt to find a legal way out, Mandela assumed his full responsibility. This conferred a new status of moral dignity on his leadership, which became evident from the moment he was returned to Robben Island. Even on his first arrival, two years before, he had set an example by refusing to obey an order to jog from the harbor, where the ferry docked, to the prison gates. The warden in charge warned him bluntly that unless he started obeying, he might quite simply be killed and that no one on the

'I have fought against white domination; I have fought against black domination. [The ideal of a free society] is an ideal which I hope to live for and to achieve. But, if needs be, it is an ideal for which I am prepared to die.'

—NELSON MANDELA

mainland would ever be the wiser. Whereupon Mandela quietly retorted, "If you so much as lay a hand on me, I will take you to the highest court in the land, and when I finish with you, you will be as poor as a church mouse." Amazingly, the warden backed off. "Any man or institution that tries to rob me of my dignity will lose," Mandela later wrote in notes smuggled out by friends.

His major response to the indignities of the prison was a creative denial of victimhood, expressed most remarkably by a system of self-education, which earned the prison the appellation of "Island University." As the prisoners left their cells in the morning to toil in the extremes of summer and winter, buffeted by the merciless southeaster or broiled by the African sun (whose glare in the limestone quarry permanently impaired Mandela's vision), each team was assigned an instructor—in history, economics, politics, philosophy, whatever. Previously barren recreation hours were filled with cultural activities, and Mandela recalls with pride his acting in the role of Creon in Sophocles' *Antigone*.

After more than two decades in prison, confident that on some crucial issues a leader must make decisions on his own, Mandela decided on a new approach. And after painstaking preliminaries, the most famous prisoner in the world was escorted, in the greatest secrecy, to the State President's office to start negotiating not only his own release but also the nation's transition from apartheid to democracy. On Feb. 2, 1990, President F.W. de Klerk lifted the ban on the ANC. and announced Mandela's imminent release.

Then began the real test. Every inch of the way, Mandela had to win the support of his own followers. More difficult still was the process of allaying white fears. But the patience, the wisdom, the visionary quality Mandela brought to his struggle, and above all the moral integrity with which he set about to unify a divided people, resulted in the country's first

'Let the strivings of us all prove Martin Luther King Jr,. to have been correct, when he said that humanity can no longer be tragically bound to the starless midnight of racism and war.'

—NELSON MANDELA

democratic elections and his selection as President.

The road since then has not been easy. Tormented by the scandals that pursued his wife Winnie, from whom he finally parted; plagued by corruption among his followers; dogged by worries about delivering on programs of job creation and housing in a country devastated by white greed, he has become a sadder, wiser man.

In the process he has undeniably made mistakes, based on a stubborn belief in himself. Yet his stature and integrity remain such that these failings tend to enhance rather than diminish his humanity. Camus once said one man's chains imply that we are all enslaved; Mandela proves through his own example that faith, hope and charity are qualities attainable by humanity as a whole. Through his willingness to walk the road of sacrifice, he has reaffirmed our common potential to move toward a new age.

And he is not deluded by the adulation of the world. Asked to comment on the BBC's unflattering verdict on his performance as a leader, Mandela said with a smile, "It helps to make you human."

'Nelson Mandela is a tiger for our time. And the tiger has come home to claim his natural habitat in Africa. Nelson Mandela has achieved the impossible.'

—ANDRÉ BRINK

elizabeth cady stanton

by Bruce Miroff

A T THE FIRST WOMEN'S RIGHTS CONVENTION in America, held in her home town of Seneca Falls, New York, in 1848, Elizabeth Cady Stanton discovered the vocation that would shape the remainder of her life. She would become a public voice for women's grievances and a prophet of genuine equality between the sexes. Battling for this vocation against the ridicule of men, the fears of women, and the continuing claims of her own family upon her, she emerged after the Civil War as the most vocal agitator and the most penetrating thinker in the ranks of nineteenth-century American feminists. Stanton's subsequent public career was not without disturbing episodes. The pain of women's exclusion from the rights of citizenship led her, on occasion, to outbursts of nativist and racist sentiments. Yet her career was always animated by a profound

Elizabeth Cady Stanton was born in Johnstown, NY in 1815 and was involved in abolitionist and women's suffragist movements. In 1840 Stanton attended the World Anti-Slavery Convention in London, protesting the exclusion of women from the assembly. After the Civil War, Stanton focused exclusively on all facets of women's rights in the United States, publishing <u>Revolution</u>, a weekly paper, from 1868-69, and founding the National Woman Suffrage Association with Susan B. Anthony in 1869.

'Stanton, a frus-
trated 33-year-old
mother of three
sons, poured out
the torrent of her
long accumulating
discontent with
such vehemence,
she stirred
herself...to do or
dare anything.'

—BARBARA GOLDSMITH

insight into women's subjugation and a passionate commitment to the freedom of all women.

Prior to the convention at Seneca Falls, Elizabeth Cady Stanton had struggled unsuccessfully against the dominant social convention of "separate spheres," which reserved the fields of politics and business for men, while restricting women to the "sphere" of domesticity. She was born in 1815 in Johnstown, New York. Her mother was a strong woman, but it was Elizabeth's father, a wealthy landowner and judge, who exercised the decisive influence on her childhood.

Although Elizabeth's father insisted that her life follow a conventional path of marriage and domesticity, he could not prevent her from following that path into unconventional circles. Making frequent visits to the Peterboro, New York, home of her older cousin, Gerrit Smith, a prominent antislavery leader, she came into contact with numerous abolitionists and other reformers who congregated under the hospitable Smith's roof. Among these was Henry Stanton, a romantic young abolitionist agitator whom she married in 1840. [However], she began to view her confinement in their home as representative; her own hunger for a larger life as a metaphor for women's hunger for political and social equality. The slogan of the modern women's movement—"the personal is political"—would have come as no surprise to Stanton. From her personal discontent with women's restricted "sphere," she derived a fundamental insight into an oppression that needed to be combatted through political action. Stanton had ample amounts of the frustration, passion, and vision necessary for the founding of a feminist politics in America. All that she lacked was a catalyst.

That catalyst was Lucretia Mott. Stanton had become friendly with Mott, a pioneer abolitionist and feminist, at an international antislavery gathering in London in 1840. The two had been outraged by the overwhelming majority vote at this convention to exclude women as delegates, and had talked of convening a meeting to discuss women's rights as soon as they returned to America. Although this plan was not carried out, Stanton remained in touch with Mott, whom she came to look upon as her mentor and role model. In the summer of 1848, Mott came on a visit to Waterloo, a town near Seneca Falls. Meeting there with her and three other women on July 13, 1848, Stanton knew that at last she had a sympathetic audience for her rebellious thoughts. As she recalled in her autobiography, *Eighty years and More*, "I poured out, that day, the torrent of my long-accumulating discontent, with such vehemence and indignation that I stirred myself, as well as the rest of the party, to do and dare anything. . . . We decided, then and there, to call a 'Woman's Rights Convention'. . . ."

On July 19, 1848, only six days after Stanton had poured out her personal discontents, the first women's rights convention began. The hastily organized convention was well attended. Several hundred women and several dozen men came from a radius of fifty miles to the small Wesleyan chapel at Seneca Falls to hear Stanton and her colleagues proclaim a new struggle for female equality. The response of the audience was favorable; at the conclusion of the convention, sixty-eight women and thirty-two men signed the resolutions that Stanton had prepared.

Stanton's speech at the convention refuted every ground—physical, intellectual, moral—for men's self-proclaimed superiority over women. This speech was more, however, than a brief for women's equality; it was also a personal declaration of vocation. Propelling herself from domesticity to public activity in a single leap, Stanton made herself into a political voice for her sex.

With the Seneca Falls convention of 1848, Elizabeth Cady Stanton began a public career that would span more than half a century. But before she could fully come into her own as a feminist leader, she would have to surmount a series of formidable obstacles. The first of these obstacles was the ridicule of men. In her speech at the convention, Stanton had

'I revolted in spirit against the customs of society and the laws of the state that crushed my aspirations and debarred me from the pursuit of every object worthy of an intelligent, rational mind.'

—ELIZABETH CADY STANTON

> 'The history of mankind is a history of repeated injuries and usurpations on the part of man towards women.'
>
> —ELIZABETH CADY STANTON

predicted that the women's protest would raise a storm. But she and her colleagues were unprepared for the sarcastic contempt with which their handiwork was greeted. Newspapers throughout the nation vied in lampooning the Seneca Falls declaration and resolutions. And they sharply reproached Stanton and her colleagues for forgetting their proper "sphere." In the words of a Philadelphia paper: "A woman is a nobody. A wife is everything. A pretty girl is equal to ten thousand men, and a mother is, next to God, all powerful. . . ."

The obstacles to Stanton's feminist leadership were also closer to home. She was a founding mother of the women's rights movement in a literal as well as a figurative sense; by 1859, she had seven children to bind her to the domestic sphere. Her husband, frequently absent on legal and political business, expected her to stay at home and place maternal and household cares above feminist endeavors. Her father, the person whose approval she wanted most desperately, warned her that she would pay an emotional and financial price for her public voice, threatening to disinherit her if she became a feminist lecturer. (He carried through with the threat, but later relented.) Loving her children intensely, glorying in her experiences as a mother, Stanton still repeatedly lamented the restricted public role that seemed to be the concomitant of her motherhood. Writing to Susan B. Anthony in 1852, she cried out: "I am at the boiling point! If I do not find some day the use of my tongue on this question, I shall die of an intellectual repression, a woman's rights convulsion!"

Shortly before she turned fifty, Stanton shed the remaining constraints of domesticity—there were no more babies to bind her to home—and took up a full-time public career amid the heated political atmosphere of the Civil War and Reconstruction. Once the dominant political forces of the Reconstruction era began to promote the rights of black men, while ignoring the rights of the women who had labored for their emancipation, she threw herself into what was to be the most painful episode in her entire public life. In the name of a passionate and outraged defense of women's rights, Stanton broke with her former abolitionist and radical Republican allies, and opposed passage of the Fourteenth and Fifteenth Amendments because they excluded women. She went beyond principled opposition to black manhood suffrage to articulate a racist and nativist position that violated her own egalitarian convictions. Fighting for women's cause with every weapon at her command, she helped to shape a more autonomous women's movement—but at a heavy cost to her own domestic vision.

The three decades remaining to Stanton after Reconstruction, up to her death in 1902, were filled with the vigorous public activities of a feminist agitator. In the 1870s, her principal role was as a traveling lecturer, spreading her feminist views across the nation. In the 1880s, she joined with Susan B. Anthony and Matilda Joslyn Gage to compile the multivolume *History of Woman Suffrage*, preserving the words and deeds of early feminists for later generations. During the final years of her life, she became convinced that religious teachings about the inferiority of women stood in the way of equality between the sexes, and produced *The Woman's Bible*, as a critical commentary on the biblical depiction of women. This work was repudiated by an increasingly conservative and Christian women's movement, leaving the elderly Stanton isolated but proudly defiant in her prophetic feminist militancy.

Elizabeth Cady Stanton could be self-righteous in her feminist individualism. Her proud self-assertion sometimes conveyed an air of superiority. But the principal force in her public life was always a sense of outrage at the degradation of women and an empathy for all women confronting that degradation. The individualist who plumbed her own "solitude of self" never forgot her bond to the multitudes of women whose redemption she once described as her "whole-souled, all-absorbing, agonizing interest."

'Stanton was the founding genius of the women's rights movement, brilliant, insightful and eloquent.'

—NATIONAL WOMEN'S HALL OF FAME

ho chi minh

by David Halberstam

O CHI MINH WAS ONE OF THE EXTRAORDINARY figures of this era—part Gandhi, part Lenin, all Vietnamese. He was, perhaps more than any single man of the century, the living embodiment to his own people— and to the world—of their revolution. He was an old Bolshevik and a founding member of the French Communist party (what could be more alien to the average Vietnamese peasant?); yet to most Vietnamese peasants he was the symbol of their existence, their hopes, their struggles, their sacrifices and their victories. (Even after Dienbienphu, when many people of North Vietnam became angry with the Communist regime, they were always careful to exclude Ho from their blame: the Communists were responsible for the bad things—Ho, Uncle Ho, for the good things.) He was a more senior mem-

Ho Chi Minh was born in Kim-Lien, North Vietnam, in 1892. Largely educated in socialist and communist politics while he lived in France, Ho remained in exile from Vietnam, travelling extensively until 1940. After nine years of fighting, he defeated the French colonialists in 1954 and became president of North Vietnam until his death in 1969.

ber of the Communist world than Mao, and he grouped around him an impressive assemblage of brilliant young men; he went through revolution, war, postwar development and another war without the slightest touch of purge. The Vietnamese Communist party remained to a unique degree a constant, mainly (according to students of its history) because of the dominating quality of its leader, for he combined total commitment with both tactical and long-range political skill.

Yet to the population he was always the symbol they needed: he was the gentle Vietnamese, humble, soft-spoken, mocking his own position, always seen in the simplest garb, his dress making him barely distinguishable from the poorest peasant—a style that Westerners for many years mocked, laughing at the lack of trappings of power, of uniform, of style, until one day they woke up and realized that this very simplicity, this cult of simplicity, this capacity to walk simply among his own people was basic to his success. In contrast, wrote Graham Greene in 1956 about Ngo Dinh Diem, the American-sponsored leader in the South, "He is separated from the people by cardinals and police cars with wailing sirens and foreign advisors droning of global strategy when he should be walking in the rice fields unprotected, learning the hard way how to be loved and obeyed— the two cannot be separated . . ."

Time magazine, the purest expression of Christian capitalism, in 1948 referred to Ho contemptuously as "goat-bearded," a "Mongoloid Trotsky" and a "tubercular agitator who learned his trade in Moscow." But it was that very same contempt—which every peasant in Vietnam felt from every Westerner—that would make him so effective. This was Ho's great strength, the fact that he was a Vietnamese Everyman, and it was why he shunned monuments and marshals' uniforms and generals' stars, for he had dealt with powerful Westerners all his life, had surely been offered countless bribes by them, but he had chosen not to be like them, not to dress

'I want every Vietnamese to have food to eat, a shirt to wear, and his children to have an education.'

—HO CHI MINH

like them or live like them. Rather, he remained a Vietnamese, a peasant, a man like one's ancestors—pure, uncorrupted in a corrupting world, a man of the land and its simple virtues.

In a country where the population had seen leaders reach a certain plateau and then become more Western and less Vietnamese, corrupted by Western power and money and ways, and where, the moment they had risen far enough to do anything for their own people, immediately sold out to the foreigners, the simplicity of Ho was powerful stuff. The higher he rose, the simpler and purer Ho seemed, always retaining the eternal Vietnamese values: respect for old people, disdain for money, affection for children. In 1951 in the middle of the war he could close a meeting of the Vietnamese Communist party by telling the gathering: "About a revolutionary man and a revolutionary party, the great Chinese writer Lu-Hsun has this couplet:

He stares disdainfully upon a thousand athletes,

And bows to serve as a horse to children.

"'Thousand athletes,'" he would then explain, "means powerful enemies like the French colonialists and the American interventionists, or difficulties and hardships. 'Children' means the peaceful masses of people, or deeds beneficent to the State and the party."

By his leadership and brilliance, Ho helped transform an era. In the twenties and thirties, he was one of the chief verbal critics of colonialism, a lonely and usually ignored voice. In the fifties, he was responsible for putting together the political and military machinery that led an underdeveloped peasantry in a successful revolutionary war against a powerful Western nation—a war that ended not only the French dominance over Vietnam but the mystique of white supremacy and colored inferiority throughout the colonial world. It also jarred a generation of Westerners out of the basic confidence in their ideas and institutions; jarred them out of the

'They see Marx isn't real to life, so what do they believe in? Many have found the answer in Ho Chi Minh Thought.'

—SON

'France under-
valued the power
Ho wielded. There's
no doubt that
he aspired to
become the Gandhi
of Indochina.'

—JEAN SAINTENY

automatic assumption that these were the best of all possible ideas, that it was only a matter of transplanting them from Europe and America, where they had flourished, and diligently applying them to Asia and Africa. What Ho set forth in his successful revolutionary war against the French and his war against the Americans had enormous impact on the West and on the underdeveloped world. And in the West the younger generation particularly would understand and sympathize with what Ho had done far more than their parents did. Indeed, even while America was fighting Ho's troops, the American paperback edition of his writings, *Ho Chi Minh on Revolution* would claim, "Written in prison, exile, and battle, this is the political bible followed by half the world."

Much of his life was cloaked in the anonymity that any Asian possessed, as far as Westerners were concerned, at the turn of the century. But he had as well the additional anonymity that goes with an underground figure—staying one step ahead of the police of several nations, changing his name regularly (at one point it was believed that he had died in a Hong Kong jail), then returning to his own nation to lead an underground revolution, this time from the mountains, so that even his wartime acts and decisions were curiously private and secret. Even in the Communist world more is normally known about leaders; Tito, Stalin, Khrushchev, Mao—all had their cult of personality.

But Ho deliberately did not seek the trappings of power and authority, as if he were so sure of himself and his relationship to both his people and history that he did not need statues and bridges, books and photographs to prove it to him or them. One sensed in him such a remarkable confidence about who he was, what he had done, that there would be no problem communicating it to his people; indeed, to try to communicate it by any artificial means might have created doubts among them. His abstinence from his own cult was particularly remarkable in the underdeveloped world, where the jump from poor peasant to ruler of a nation in a brief span of time often proves very heady stuff and inspires more than the predictable quota of self-commemoration.

In his lifetime Ho had not only liberated his own country and changed the course of colonial rule in both Africa and Asia, he had done something even more remarkable; he had touched the culture and the soul of his enemy. For goat-bearded, Mongoloid-Trotsky, tubercular agitator Ho Chi Minh, it had been a full life.

'All my life, I have served the Father-land, the revolution and its people with all my heart and strength. If I should depart now from this world, I would regret nothing.'

—HO CHI MINH

václav havel

by Peter C. Newman

ONLY MET HIM ONCE, but I've never forgotten my few private moments with Vaclav Havel, the secular saint who last week fell critically ill in Prague and, according to his doctors, may not recover.

Our brief meeting took place in Ottawa in 1990, when he was on his way to Washington to address a joint session of Congress, and he didn't have much time. But he was glad to meet someone who could speak Czech, so he wouldn't have to rely on his interpreter. (She was a tiny Oriental woman he kept tucked under his left shoulder, who was so good at her job that as local well-wishers talked to him, she would whisper to Havel in Czech, lip read his answer and reply almost instantaneously in perfect Oxford English.)

From our brief exchange, I recall only two fragments. "I've learned never to be surprised by anything," he

Václav Havel **was born in Prague in 1936 and became a playwright whose works were banned in Czechoslovakia under the Communist regime. In 1977 Havel banded together with other "dissidents" to write Charter 77, calling for civil and human rights to be respected in Czechoslovakia, and then in 1979 Havel wrote his famous revolutionary essay, "The Power of the Powerless." After the Velvet Revolution in 1989, Havel was elected president of Czechoslovakia, and then elected president of the newly formed Czech Republic in 1993.**

shrugged, when I asked how it felt for a beleaguered playwright to suddenly find himself a famous president. To my question about the secret of politics, he shot back: "Write your own way." Then he paused, and added: "Of course, everyone is replaceable."

I'm not so sure.

Havel was one of those rare conscience-driven politicians we can't afford to lose. He kept himself removed from the darker tricks of his craft and was never impressed by the fumes of fame. Havel believed that character is destiny and that it was therefore essential to live a principled life, even at the risk of being imprisoned for his beliefs—which he was.

A scruffy man with originally ginger-colored hair and an orange moustache (one friend joked, "Vaclav looks as if carrot juice is flowing through his veins"), he enjoyed a highly developed sense of the absurd. His plays were absurdist creations in mundane settings with universal characters. Havel started writing when he was 13, but Czech theatre was closed to him until the Velvet Revolution of 1989.

He led the peaceful overthrow of the occupying Russians and in the winter of 1989 assumed Czechoslovakia's presidency. That meant moving into Hradcany Castle, a huge pile of palaces and cathedrals overlooking the Vltava River, which bisects Prague. Just eight months earlier, he had been serving a four-year sentence in a Communist prison a few kilometers away.

He had been the spiritual catalyst of the bloodless revolt that swept the Communists out of power, and now he was the country's first democratic president since 1938. Being a playwright, one of the first things Havel did was to make sure everyone wore appropriate costumes. He asked his friend Theodor Pistek (who won an Academy Award for his costumes in the movie *Amadeus*) to design properly pretentious royal blue parade uniforms—complete with toy sabres—for the castle guards. When they were

'You do not become a "dissident" just because you decide one day to take up this most unusual career.'

—VACLAV HAVEL

delivered, Havel tried one on, and bellowing "Let's go scare the cooks!" ran into the castle kitchens, waving his pretend weapon. He later got fed up with soldiers marching around the castle to regal marching music and had one of his friends compose a jarring melody in seven-eighths time that no one could possibly march to, then insisted it be played for the changing of the guard ceremonies. Hradcany Castle is so huge that Havel sometimes resorted to getting around the place on a scooter, and after the first few weeks in office he agreed not to come to work in jeans and received visitors wearing a polka-dot tie. (His first press secretary was Michael Zantovsky, whose only claim to fame was as the author of the only study in Czech of the films of Woody Allen.)

As president (he was re-elected in 1990 and 1993), Havel granted amnesty to 30,000 prisoners, presided over the peaceful withdrawal of Soviet troops, defied public opinion by supporting the reunification of Germany, masterminded the Czech Republic's NATO application, and brought some badly needed enlightenment to a country that had not known democracy since 1938.

But his main contributions were his evocative speeches, written by himself on a manual typewriter. Probably the best was his 1990 New Year's message:

> For 40 years, on this day, you heard the same thing in different variations from my predecessors: how our country flourished, how many million tons of steel we produced, how happy we all were, how we trusted our government and what bright perspectives were unfolding in front of us.
>
> I assume you did not nominate me to this office so that I, too, would lie to you.
>
> Our country is not flourishing. The enormous creative and spiritual potential of our nations is not being used sensibly.

'Like his predecessor Thomas Jefferson, Havel is a politician with the soul of a writer and a writer with the savvy of a politician.'

—GEORGE STEPHANOPOULIS

Entire branches of industry are producing goods that are of no interest to anyone. A country that once could be proud of the educational level of its citizens spends so little time on education that it ranks today as 72nd in the world. We have contaminated the soil, rivers and forests bequeathed to us by our ancestors, and today we have the most polluted environment in Europe. Adults in our country die earlier than in most other European countries.

Allow me a little personal observation: When I flew to Bratislava recently, I found time during various discussions to look out of the plane window. I saw the industrial complex of the Slovnaft chemical factory and the giant Petrzalka housing estate right behind it. The view was enough to make me realize that for decades our statesmen and political leaders did not look or did not want to look out of the windows of their airplanes. . . .

He went on like that for about 10 minutes, then came to his seminal point: "Let us teach both ourselves and others that politics does not have to be the art of the possible, especially if this means the art of intrigues, secret agreements, and pragmatic maneuverings. But that it can also be the art of the impossible, that is the art of making both ourselves and the world better."

"You may ask me what kind of a republic I dream of. Let me reply: I dream of a republic independent, free, and democratic, of a republic economically prosperous and yet socially just; in short, of a humane republic which serves the individual and which therefore holds the hope that the individual will serve it in turn. Of a republic of well-rounded people, because without such it is impossible to solve any of our problems, human, economic, ecological, social, or political.

The most distinguished of my predecessors opened his first speech with a quotation from the great Czech educator

'In the Prague spring of 1968, a celebrated young playwright boldly called for an end to one-party rule before Soviet tanks crushed hopes. Vaclav Havel's plays were banned. He lost his job, but he carried on.'

—BILL CLINTON

Comenius. Allow me to close my first speech with my own paraphrase of the same statement:

People, your government has returned to you!"

"Man," Havel once wrote from jail, "is nailed down—like Christ on the cross—to a grid of paradoxes. He balances between the torment of not knowing his mission and the joy of carrying it out."

'The dissident...is not seeking power. He offers nothing and promises nothing. He can offer, if anything, only his own skin—and he offers it solely because he has no other way of affirming the truth he stands for.'

—VACLAV HAVEL

cesar chavez

by Peter Matthiessen

ESAR CHAVEZ WAS ON UNION BUSINESS when his life ended quietly in his sleep, at 10:30 or 11 p.m. on April 22nd, in the small border town of San Luis, Arizona, thirty-five miles and sixty-six years distant from the childhood farm in the Gila River Valley which his parents lost at the end of the Depression. On April 29th, in ninety-degree heat, an estimated thirty-five thousand people, in a line three miles long, formed a funeral procession from Memorial Park in Delano, California, to the burial Mass, at the United Farm Workers field office north of town.

With the former scourge of California safely in his coffin, state flags were lowered to half-mast by order of the governor, and messages poured forth from the heads of church and state, including the Pope and the President of the United States. This last of the U.F.W. marches was

---

Cesar Chavez, born 1927 in Yuma, Arizona, was a community organizer and leader of migrant farmworkers. In 1962, he formed the National Farm Workers Association, which would become the United Farm Workers. Famous for his successful boycott of grapes that led to improved working conditions for migrant grape pickers, Chavez died in 1993.

'There's no turning back....We will win. We are winning because ours is a revolution of mind and heart.'

—CESAR CHAVEZ

greater, even, than the 1975 march against the Gallo winery, which helped destroy the growers' cynical alliance with the Teamsters. "We have lost perhaps the greatest Californian of the twentieth century," the president of the California State Senate said, in public demotion of Cesar Chavez's sworn enemies Nixon and Reagan.

For most of his life, Cesar Estrada Chavez chose to live penniless and without property, devoting everything he had, including his frail health, to the U.F.W., the first effective farmworkers' union ever created in the United States. "Without a union, the people are always cheated, and they are so innocent," Chavez told me when we first met, in July, 1968, in Delano, where he lived with his wife, Helen, and a growing family. Chavez, five feet six, and a sufferer from recurrent back pain, seemed an unlikely David to go up against the four-billion-dollar Goliath of California agribusiness. Not until January, 1968, after many hard years of door-to-door organizing of uneducated and intimidated migrant workers, had his new independent union felt strong enough to attempt a nationwide boycott of table grapes, publicized by the first of many prolonged religious fasts. On July 29, 1970, the main Delano growers all but ended the boycott by signing union contracts with the U.F.W.

This historic victory was no sooner won when the U.F.W. was challenged by the Teamsters Union, which rushed in to sign up lettuce workers in the Salinas Valley. Chavez was angered by the perfidy of the growers, who were bent on conspiring with the Teamsters to steal from behind the U.F.W.'s back what it had won in a fair, hard fight. He also resented the hostility of almost all municipal and state officials, from the ubiquitous police to Governor Reagan, which exposed his farmworkers to an unrestrained climate of violence and took the lives of five U.F.W. members in the course of strikes and organizing campaigns. For Chavez, that hostility led to a resurfacing of emotional injuries he had suffered as a child, all the way back to the bank foreclosure on the small family farm and the brutal racism in such signs as "No Dogs or Mexicans Allowed." "Getting rejected hurts very deep," he told me once, recalling a time in Indio, California, during his migrant days when he followed his father into a decrepit diner to buy morning coffee, only to be contemptuously ordered out. To this day, he said, he could remember the expression on his father's face, and though it has been twenty years or more since Cesar told me that story, I can still recall his expression when he told it—that seraphic Indian face with the dark, sad, soft eyes and delighted smile turned crude and ugly.

In recent years, beset by the unremitting prejudice of California's Republican administrations, which were elected with the strong support of agribusiness, the embittered Chavez embarked upon a table-grape and lettuce boycott against nonunion growers, protesting the use of dangerous pesticides, which threaten the health not only of farmworkers but of the public. The new boycott never took hold. What was lacking seemed to be the fervor of those exhilarating marches under union flags, the fasts, the singing, and the chanting—"*Viva la huelga!*"—that put the fear of God in the rich farm owners of California. These brilliant tactics remained tied in the public perception to La Causa, a labor and civil-rights movement with religious overtones which rose to prominence in the feverish tumult of the sixties; as a mature A.F.L.-C.I.O union, the U.F.W. lost much of its symbolic power. Membership has now declined to about one-fifth of its peak of a hundred thousand.

With the funeral march over, the highway empty, and all the banners put away, Cesar Chavez's friends and perhaps his foes are wondering what will become of the U.F.W. A well-trained new leadership (his son-in-law has been named to succeed him, and four of his eight children work for the union) may bring fresh energy and insight. But what the union will miss is Chavez's spiritual fire. A man so unswayed by money, a man who

'Chavez is one of the heroic figures of our time.'

—ROBERT KENNEDY

'Cesar is living proof that the poor do not lack leadership, courage or a future.'

—JOSE BURCIAGA

(despite many death threats) refused to let his bodyguards go armed, and who offered his entire life to the service of others, was not to be judged by the same standards of some self-serving labor leader or politician. Self-sacrifice lay at the very heart of the devotion he inspired, and gave dignity and hope not only to the farmworkers but to every one of the Chicano people, who saw for themselves what one brave man, indifferent to his own health and welfare, could accomplish. . . .

Until Chavez appeared, union leaders had considered it impossible to organize seasonal farm labor, which is in large part illiterate and indigent, rarely remains in one place long enough to form an effective unit, and is composed mostly of minority groups that invite hostility from local communities. In consequence, strikes, protests, and unions had been broken with monotonous efficiency—a task made easier by the specific exclusion of farm workers from the protection of the National Labor Relations Act, which authorizes and regulates collective bargaining between management and labor. In a state where cheap labor, since Indian days, has been taken for granted, like the sun, reprisals were swift and sometimes fatal, and the struggles of Mexican-American farm workers for better conditions have met with defeat after defeat. . . .

The fast began on February 14, 1968, just after Chavez returned from a fund-raising tour around the country. Everywhere he had gone, the militant groups that supported him or sought his support had been talking about the violence that was being planned for the summer of 1968, and in Delano his own people were rivaling the growers with loose talk about quick solutions. It was winter, in the hungry time between the pruning and the girdling of vines, and the grape strike had been going on for two and a half years, and the workers were muttering that they had waited long enough. Hadn't violence worked in the ghetto riots of 1967? Perhaps a little burning in Delano, or an explosion or two might force the growers to negotiate. . . . Depressed, he decided on the fast as a kind of penance for the belligerence that had developed in his own union. . . .

Anger was part of Chavez, but so was a transparent love of humankind. The gentle mystic that his disciples wished to see inhabited the same small body as the relentless labor leader who concerned himself with the most minute operation of his union. Astonishingly—this seems to me his genius—the two Cesars were so complementary that without either, La Causa could not have survived.

On the twenty-first day of the fast, Chavez's physician, Dr. James McKnight, insisted that he take medication, and also wanted him to drink a few ounces of bouillon and unsweetened grapefruit juice. Dr. McKnight and many other people felt that Chavez might be doing himself permanent harm. Chavez did not agree. "After the fast, they gave me a complete analysis—blood and all that stuff—and do you know something?" Chavez smiled, shaking his head. "I was perfect!"

During the vigil at the open casket on the day before the funeral, an old man lifted a child up to show him the small, gray-haired man who lay inside. "I'm going to tell you about this man someday," he said.

'It is my deepest belief that only by giving our lives do we find life. The truest act of courage, the strongest act of manliness, is to sacrifice ourselves for others in a non-violent struggle for justice.'

—CESAR CHAVEZ

rosa luxemburg

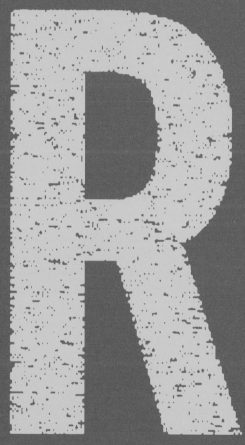

by Stephen Eric Bronner

OSA LUXEMBURG WAS BORN IN THE SMALL Polish city of Zamosc in 1871, the year of the Paris Commune. Her father was a middle-class Jew who was cosmopolitan in his views. Thus, he found Zamosc somewhat stifling and moved his family to Warsaw in 1873, the year in which Rosa would develop the hip affliction that would remain with her for the rest of her life. A Jew in Poland who spoke German at home, Rosa learned of Schiller, the Enlightenment, and cosmopolitanism in her family circle. . . .

It was in high school that Rosa Luxemburg first became politically active. During this time she made the acquaintance of Martin Kasprzak, a founder of socialism in Poland, who was to die on the scaffold in 1905. She also joined the Proletariat party, which, like most of the East European socialist parties before the turn of the century,

Rosa Luxemburg, born in Russian Poland in 1871, became a German citizen in 1895 and then emigrated to Zurich in 1889. A theorist, writer, prophet of socialism, and founding member of the German Communist Party, she was arrested and murdered by German soldiers after the Sparticist rebellion in Berlin in 1919.

was highly centralized and patterned somewhat after the famous and terroristic Russian Narodnaya Volya (People's Will). Soon enough, Proletariat came under police surveillance and harassment. Thus, after leaving high school in 1887, Rosa Luxemburg escaped to Zurich. There she began her socialist apprenticeship in earnest; she read Marx and Engels for the first time and entered into the world of radical emigré life with its endless cafe colloquies, personal quarrels, and intense intellectual friendships. It was also in Zurich that she met her future lover and political mentor Leo Jogiches. The meeting would result in a stormy and intense relationship that would come to an abrupt end around 1906 — 1907, though their political collaboration was to last until Rosa's death in the midst of the Spartacus rebellion of 1919.

And then too, Zurich offered her its university. There Rosa would study mathematics, natural science, and political economy. Particularly in prison, she returned again and again to studying the natural sciences, although her central concern was always political economy. Rosa Luxemburg was immediately recognized as a brilliant student and her dissertation on the industrial development of Poland, written under the tutelage of Julius Wolf, received the rare honor (at that time) of being published as a book.

Its argument served as a complement to and theoretical justification of the political position she had taken as early as her high school years. Rosa Luxemburg had always been opposed to a socialism that advocated Polish nationalism, and her dissertation sought to show that Polish industrial development was dependent upon the growth of the Russian market and Russian capitalism. This insight led her to stress the need for solidarity between Polish and Russian workers and to reject the need for Polish separatism.

The unity between the theoretical in Rosa Luxemburg's writing and the concrete needs of political practice formed early, and it was never broken. In concrete terms, the political implications that she drew from her

'There are few monuments to the socialist pursuit of freedom, but the life of Rosa Luxemburg is one of them.'

—STEPHEN BRONNER

economic research served as the theoretical basis for the journal *Sprawa Robotnicza* (*The Workers' Voice*), which Luxemburg and Jogiches founded in 1893. That same year, a strike wave encompassing 60,000 workers hit the city of Lodz. In the wake of these events, the Proletariat party joined with the Polish Workers' League to form the Socialist Party of Poland (PPS). This was the party that would fall more and more under the direction of the two men who were to become Rosa Luxemburg's arch-enemies within the movement for Polish socialism, Ignaz Daszynski and Josef Pilsudski. Like Mussolini, Pilsudski would later defect from socialism altogether and become the dictator of Poland in the twenties. It was this attempt to steer the PPS into the nationalist camp that led Luxemburg to support a new party that would oppose the PPS: the Social Democratic Party of the Kingdom of Poland and Lithuania (SDKPL), the party to which she would devote herself for the rest of her life.

Rosa Luxemburg's critique of nationalism still retains a fundamental validity. Indeed, her analysis assumes importance both in terms of those revolutionary values that the contemporary Left seeks to foster and in regard to the type of society that it wishes to actualize. For Rosa Luxemburg saw that nationalism would chain the socialist movement to the ideology of that bourgeois class it seeks to oppose. She also realized that a purely "national" revolution would undermine socialism by tying the nation to a bourgeois economy that was becoming ever more interdependent and transnational. Finally, and perhaps most important, the simple acceptance of a nationalistic consciousness would necessarily prevent the proletariat from recognizing the fact that the nation state and nationalism are strictly historical phenomena that might, at any given time, become obsolete. The emphasis upon nationalism would thus effectively deny the possibility of creating an alternative to the bourgeois form of socioeconomic organization and cripple the ability of the workers' movement to conceptu-

'Freedom for the members of one party—no matter how numerous they may be— is no freedom at all. Freedom is always and exclusively freedom for the one who thinks differently.'

—ROSA LUXEMBURG

alize the common humanity remained central to serve. Toward the end of her life she would write to [her friend] Mathilde Wurm:

> What do you want with this particular suffering of the Jews? The poor victims on the rubber plantations in Putamayo, the Negroes in Africa with whose bodies the Europeans play a game of catch, are just as near to me. Do you remember the words written on the work of the Great General Staff about Trotha's campaign in the Kalahari desert? "and the death-rattles, the mad cries of those dying of thirst, faded away into the sublime silence of eternity."
>
> Oh, this "sublime silence of eternity" in which so many screams have faded away unheard. It rings within me so strong that I have no special corner of my heart reserved for the ghetto: I am at home wherever in the world there are clouds, birds and human tears.

Few individuals—Trotsky would be one of them—ever rose to fame in the socialist world as quickly as did Rosa Luxemburg. Still, she had to earn her spurs as a party worker, and thus it was that in 1898 the SPD sent her to Poznan—an area that she called "the boundary between civilization and barbarism" in one of her letters—to organize the Polish workers living on German soil. Traveling in the area proved exhausting, the incessant meetings tiring, and the organizational work mundane. Yet it all seemed to serve a function, even though the SPD was actually only using the SDKPL in its rivalry with Pilsudski's PPS.

Ultimately, the organizational efforts of both parties would prove a failure. But, with this initial trial that she bore so cheerfully, Rosa Luxemburg gained the practical credentials she needed as the party's expert on East European questions, as well as a mandate to attend the meetings of the International. Then, too, her experience was a factor when the movement chose her to sit on the commission that was to arbitrate the bitter quar-

'To be sure, terrorism indicates fundamental weakness.'

—ROSA LUXEMBURG

rel that broke out between the Bolsheviks and Mensheviks in 1902.

By 1906, the tsarist police had arrested Rosa. She faced a long prison term, but connections made it possible for her to be released on the 3,000 rubles that her father and the SPD had raised for bail. It was no secret to the authorities that she would jump bail, yet she wrote: "My friends absolutely insist that I telegraph [Premier Sergei] Witte, and that I write the German Consul here. I wouldn't think of it! These gentlemen can wait a long time before a Social Democrat asks them for protection and justice. Long live the revolution!" What emerges here is not simply inflated pride, but a perception of a social democracy that stands implacably opposed to the bourgeoisie. No quarter is to be asked from the enemy, for that friction necessary for proletarian class consciousness must continually be emphasized if the proletariat is to view itself as "sovereign."

Rosa Luxemburg's concern for democracy should not obscure this hatred of the bourgeoisie. Democracy can never be actualized under the material exploitation of the capitalist system; the exploitative system and the bourgeoisie have to be suppressed, but they can only be suppressed by the dictatorship of a class—not the dictatorship over a class by a small group of party leaders—that demands the actualization of democracy in the socioeconomic, as well as in the political, realm. Only in this manner can the sovereignty of the proletariat be assured.

It is this type of self-contained proletarian sovereignty that underlies Rosa Luxemburg's theory of the mass strike, and even of the relation between the party and the masses. The mass strike for Luxemburg was neither the apex of revolution, as it was for the anarchists, nor a "myth" in Sorel's sense. Rather, the mass strike was a stage within the revolutionary conflict itself. During that stage, the artificial division between political and economic organization could be overcome and the proletariat could begin the manifold social experiment of organizing itself in new ways.

'The truth is that even the greatest revolution can only create what is historically possible to create.'

—ROSA LUXEMBURG

michael collins

by Tim Pat Coogan

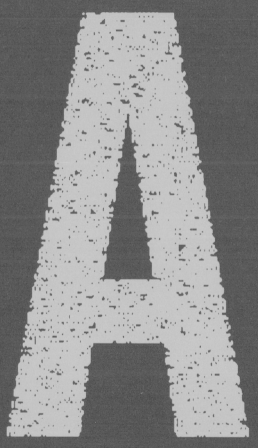

MERICA'S LOSS WAS TO BE IRELAND'S GAIN. For if Michael Collins had taken his brother Pat's advice, the Republic of Ireland might not exist today. Watching the storm clouds of World War I gather over Europe, Pat had written to Michael from Chicago urging his young brother to leave his job in a London stockbroker's office and come to join him in America. Had they teamed up, one is tempted to speculate that one of the all-time great Pat-and-Mike success stories might have resulted. But twenty-six-year-old Michael agonized over the decision while walking the docks of London, seeing the ships leave for the New World. War was imminent; a call up would surely follow, bringing with it an unthinkable choice: either become a conscientious objector or don a British uniform and fight for the Crown.

Michael Collins, born in County Cork, Ireland, in 1890, joined in the Easter uprising of 1916, and subsequently became the general of the national army in Ireland. He was largely responsible for the treaty with the British government that led to the free Irish state, and was killed in an ambush in 1922.

'This is the man
who singlehandedly
brought the
British empire
to its knees.'

— THOMAS FLANAGAN

Eventually Collins solved the problem in his own inimitable way. He put on an Irish uniform and went to fight for Ireland, in the 1916 Easter Rebellion in Dublin. That searing week of flame and folly claimed the lives of some of the people he most admired: Tom Clarke, James Connolly, Sean Hurley, Sean MacDiarmida, Joseph Plunkett. With their deaths, there also died his faith in conventional methods of fighting for Ireland's freedom. He still believed in fighting. But in the parliamentary game as played at Westminster the rules were so arranged that the outnumbered Irish nationalists always lost. Now he understood that static warfare—seizing a stronghold, be it a building such as Dublin's General Post Office, in which he fought during the rebellion, or a mountain top, and then slugging it out with rifles and shot guns against an adversary who possessed heavy artillery—would continue to provide the Irish with heroes and martyrs, and the British with victories.

Instead Collins evolved a new concept of guerilla warfare that in time would be copied by guerilla leaders all over the globe from Mao to Shamir. The Collins philosophy was based not on the capture of enemy bricks and mortar, but of its information. Traditionally Dublin Castle, the seat of British administration in Ireland, had used a network of spies and informers to infiltrate and then snuff out movements directed at securing Irish independence. Collins perfected a system of spying on the spies. Every important branch of the Castle system, whether it was banking, policing, the railways, shipping, the postal service—whatever—was infiltrated by his agents. These were not highly-trained, CIA-style operatives, but ordinary men and women, little people whom nobody had ever taken notice of before. Collins gave them a belief in themselves, a courage they did not know they possessed, and they in return gave him a complete picture of how their masters operated.

A secretary in Military Intelligence saw to it that Collins had a copy of the Colonel's orders to the Captain before he received the originals. A railway porter carried dispatches, the docker smuggled in revolvers, the detective told him who the informers were—and the Squad used the revolvers to deal with those informers. For the first time in their history the Irish had a team of assassins trained to eliminate informers. Collins demoralized the hitherto invincible Royal Irish Constabulary, the armed police force that operated from fortified barracks and held Ireland for the Crown. Inevitably more generalized warfare broke out all over the country as the British introduced new men and new methods in a vain effort to counter the guerilla tactics of Collins's Active Service Units and the Flying Columns of Volunteers, which lived on the run, eating and sleeping where they could.

Held back from making a full scale use of their Army by the force of world opinion—largely Irish-American opinion—the British tried to fight a "police war" carried on by hastily-formed forces of ex-service men and officers troubled by little discipline and less conscience. The Black and Tans and the Auxiliaries wrote new chapters of horror in the bloodstained story of the Anglo-Irish relationship. Reprisals for the activities of Collins and his colleagues included the burning of homes and creameries, random murder and the widespread use of torture. Through it all Collins lived a "life on the bicycle." The most-wanted man in Europe, he smiled his way through a hundred hold-ups never wearing a disguise, never missing an appointment, never certain where he would spend the night.

In addition to his campaign of warfare, he ran a national loan, which was banned by the British so that either its advertisement or sale became illegal. Yet the loan was fully subscribed, and every subscriber got a receipt. He was the president of the omnipresent secret society, the Irish Republican Brotherhood, which regarded him as the real president of the Irish Republic, and he was Minister for Finance in the *Sinn Fein* cabinet. In addition he was Director of Intelligence of the Irish Republican Army. Any

'My one intention is the destruction of the undesirables who continue to make miserable the life of ordinary people.... I have paid them back with their own coin.'

—MICHAEL COLLINS

'Collins wasn't a proponent of terrorism. He developed techniques of guerrilla warfare later copied by independence movements around the world.'

—NEIL JORDAN

one of those jobs would have consumed the energy of an ordinary man, but Collins combined them all efficiently and effectively.

He had little formal education (that part of his development ceased when he passed his junior-grade civil service examinations at the age of sixteen), but he was an omnivorous reader and combined a mind like a laser beam with a hawk-like eye for detail. Nothing escaped his attention. Everything attracted his interest: Shaw's latest play, the way the Swiss organized a Citizen Army, Benjamin Franklin's proposals for dealing with loyalists, or the latest edition of *Popular Mechanics*. An article in that journal in November of 1920 led to the first use in warfare of the Thomson gun. Collins saw the article on the recently-invented weapon and had enquires made about this "splendid thing," which lead to the Irish-American leader Joseph McGarrity of Philadelphia buying five hundred of the weapons. Two Irish-American ex-officers were sent to Ireland to train the I.R.A. in the use of the weapons. Only a handful got through the American customs, but these were duly used in a number of Dublin ambushes.

Tough and abrasive with his male, and sometimes female, colleagues, Collins was gentle and playful with children and old people. Throughout the eighteen months that Eamon de Valera was in America on a propaganda and fund-raising mission, Collins risked his life to call each week to his absent chief's family, bringing them money and companionship. Eventually the war effort Collins had spearheaded drove the British to a conference table and a settlement as foreseeable as it was unpalatable to many Irishmen and women; a partitioned Irish Free State that would owe allegiance to the Crown. It was a deal that had been foreshadowed to de Valera in four days of talks between himself and Lloyd George, the British Prime Minister, in London during July 1921. De Valera did not want to be the man who faced up to the implications of that deal. Instead he repaid the kindness Collins had shown his family in Machiavellian fashion. He stayed away himself from the opprobrious negotiations but manipulated Collins into going to London as part of the delegation that signed the Anglo-Irish Treaty of December 6th, 1921, the constitutional foundation document of modern Ireland. Collins took the leading part in the Treaty's negotiation. Subsequently, he became Chairman of the Executive Council (in effect, the Government) of the Irish Free State that emerged, and later Commander-in-Chief of the Army.

The Treaty did not yield the Republic he had hoped for but it provided what Collins prophetically termed a "stepping stone" to today's Irish Republic. All the other stepping stones to the tragedy of today's Northern Ireland situation were part of that negotiation too. In a very real sense Collins' premature death was caused by the forces that still rage about the Northeastern corner of the land and people for whom he fought. The story of his life explains tomorrow's news from Belfast. Would he have brought fire or prosperity to his country had he lived? Or would he have died of drink or disillusionment at the effects of the civil war that broke out over the terms of the Treaty?

We don't know. What we can be sure of is that this Irish Sigfried kept his Appointment in Samarra a couple of months short of his thirty-second birthday in a remote Cork valley known as *Beal na mBlath*, the Mouth of Flowers. He died, not far from where he was born, in an ambush laid by a former comrade in arms, a man who had undergone sadistic tortures at the hands of the British Intelligence Officers rather than betray his boyhood friend, Michael Collins. Collins' career is a paradigm of the tragedy of modern Ireland: the suffering, the waste of talent, the hope, the bedeviling effect of history and nomenclature whereby one man's terrorist is another man's freedom fighter. Like Prometheus, Collins stole fire. Like Prometheus, he paid for his feat and much of what he set about doing remains undone. But his name burns brightly wherever the Irish meet. Michael Collins was the man who made Ireland possible.

'Michael Collins is the man who made Ireland.'

— TIM PAT COOGAN

federico garcía lorca

by Roberto González

ARCÍA LORCA'S LIFE WAS HIS MOST TREASURED
artistic creation; hence there was a tragic appropriateness
to his dying as early as he did. His fascination with
death, and more obsessively with sacrifice, was such
that he would have liked his own dramatic and meaningful demise. He is one of the most famous artists vic-
timized by 20th-century politics: the child-poet who
refused to age and was crushed by pitiless history. The
story is so powerful as to be archetypal, and its retelling
is a ritual for any writer and reader, who know painfully
well its conclusion. . . .

There is a tinge of irony, even melancholy, in
the story of García Lorca's adventures—his *joie de
vivre*, the pleasures of his pampered existence as the
son of a wealthy landowner from Andalusia who

Federico García Lorca, born in Fuentevaqueros, Granada, Spain, in
1898, is considered one of that country's greatest poets and playwrights. García Lorca promoted truth in theater and writing, though he
remained on the sidelines of active political involvement. He was executed during the Spanish Civil War in 1936, and his poetry was banned
under General Francisco Franco's regime until the 1950s.

'In this world I will always be on the side of the poor. I will always be on the side of those who have nothing—those to whom even the peace of having nothing is denied.'

—FEDERICO GARCÍA LORCA

indulged his heir's fancies. His stunning successes and sudden fame mount up like a debt he will inevitably pay. Death is the canvas on which his itinerary is drawn: from Fuente Vaqueros near Granada, to Madrid, New York, Havana, Madrid, Montevideo, Buenos Aires, back to Madrid, and then, as if pulled by an irresistible force, back to Granada, where death awaited him. With Granada taken over by Franco's rebelling fascists, García Lorca sought sanctuary with the family of the poet Luis Rosales, who were members of the Falange. But not they, nor the money a desperate García Lorca offered to donate to their movement, could save him. He was shot in an obscure spot near the city, and his body (over which he had fretted so much) was never found—a final touch to the mythic figure that he became, one that grew after his death into the paradigmatic poetic life of the century.

His meteoric career was marked by success and fame, and it is a measure of the indisputable quality of his work that it was done in an extraordinarily demanding setting. He burst into the limelight in the early 1920's, when Spain was enjoying a renaissance in the arts comparable to the golden age of the 16th and 17th centuries, which saw the emergence of poets like Garcilaso de la Vega, St. John of the Cross, Fray Luis de León, Luis de Góngora and Francisco de Quevedo; novelists like Mateo Alemán and Cervantes; and playwrights like Lope de Vega, Tirso de Molina and Calderón. When García Lorca arrived in Madrid he joined the galaxy of poets that came to be known as the "generation of '27," a group that included the likes of Jorge Guillén, Vicente Aleixandre, Rafael Alberti, Gerardo Diego and Damaso Alonso. He was also in touch, sometimes intimately, with painters like Picasso and Salvador Dalí; the filmmaker Luis Bunuel and the composer Manuel de Falla.

Madrid had stolen from Paris the role as capital of the Hispanic intellectual and artistic avant-garde. García Lorca became the center of that capital—the center of the center—with his poetry, his plays and his antics in gatherings at salons and cafes.

García Lorca's achievement was based on stylizing the popular tradition, specifically Andalusian folklore and the romantic figure of the Gypsy. Interest in the Gypsy and the *cante jondo* or "deep song" was not new, but he renewed it.

This meant going back to the romance, to the ballad form that Menéndez Pidal had anointed, and which had already been the object of a similar process of stylization in Gongora three centuries earlier. Gongora's *romances artisticos*, particularly those with Moorish themes, had shown how a cultivated poet could make use of this form—not only its rhyme and meter, but also its figures and at times its odd syntax. García Lorca used word repetition to great effect. In "Romance de la Luna Luna," is the second "luna" an adjective ("ballad of the lunar moon") or just a playful, lullaby kind of iteration? And in the much-quoted opening of the "Romance sonambulo"—"verde que te quiero verde"—the mesmerizing repetition of "green" plays with the possibility that the second "verde" can be an adjective or an adverb ("I want you green" or "I want you greenly"). Shorn of melodrama and bathos, popular forms could be as stark and fresh as any devised by the most avant-garde poets. García Lorca's "Gypsy Ballads," published in 1927, became the most popular book of poetry in the Spanish language, at once a best seller and a canonical work.

García Lorca was tentative at first in the theater, but his "Blood Wedding," "Yerma," and "House of Bernarda Alba"—the

'He was a poet— a poet of the people who viewed poetry as "something that walks along the streets." '

—LESLIE STAINTON

tragic trilogy—are on a par with the best of Ibsen, Beckett, Ionesco and O'Neill. As in his poetry, in the theater García Lorca culled from the core of Spanish rural life the bare essence of tragedy. . . .

He blazed like a comet across the horizon of Hispanic literature, a poet-celebrity in the mold of his predecessor, the Nicaraguan Rubén Darío (1867—1916), who was the first to travel triumphantly from country to country accepting accolades from the powerful, and provoking the resentment of local poets. Some of those who attacked García Lorca would become famous in their own right. Jorge Luis Borges, for instance, probably irked by the way García Lorca charmed Buenos Aires into submission, acidly proclaimed him to be a "professional Andalusian" and a "minor writer." But his Spanish contemporaries, Guillén, Salinas, Alonso and even those like Alberti, with whom he had political differences, recognized his genius, as did Neruda, to whom he was linked by bonds of sincere mutual admiration. García Lorca's murder was one of the factors that pushed the Chilean poet into political activism. That murder is a crossroads in the modern history of the interplay of poetry and politics in the Hispanic world and beyond.

From his death through the 60's García Lorca was, to the world, the prototype of the Spanish poet; he and Cervantes bore the most recognizable names among writers of Spanish. But he suffered an eclipse in the past 20 years or so, replaced by Latin Americans like Borges, Octavio Paz and Gabriel García Márquez. In Latin America he was viewed as too Spanish; in Spain he was set aside after Franco's death and the advent of democracy, when he was no longer the best-known victim of the regime in power. But there is now a revival, given added impetus by the celebration

'The day hunger disappears, the world will see the greatest spiritual explosion humanity has ever seen.'

—FEDERICO GARCÍA LORCA

last year of the centenary of his birth. He is making a comeback strictly on his literary merits, no longer as a myth. This is just: discard the myth and García Lorca is still one of the greatest writers of the 20th century.

'This uncouth Andalusian poet electrified the literary world until a fascist firing squad switched him off.'

—BRIAN DAVIS

harriet tubman

by Andrew Porter

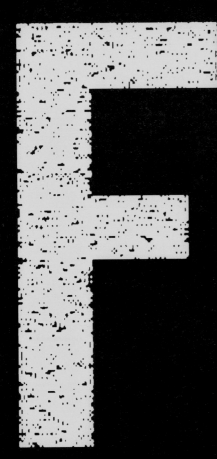

OR HER SIXTH OPERA, "Harriet, the Woman Called Moses," Thea Musgrave chose an American subject. Harriet Tubman "deserves to be placed first on the list of American heroines," said the prominent abolitionist Samuel May. In 1863, when Harriet Tubman still had fifty years to live, the Boston *Commonwealth* wrote:

> It was said long ago that the true romance of America was not in the fortunes of the Indian, where Cooper sought it, nor in New England character, where Judd [the author of "Margaret"] found it, nor in the social contrasts of Virginia planters, as Thackeray imagined, but in the story of the fugitive slaves. The observation is as true now as it was before War,

Harriet Tubman was born a slave in Buckton, Maryland, 1820. She was the most successful conductor on the Underground Railroad, personally responsible for freeing over 300 slaves, and an intelligence agent for the Union Army during the Civil War. She was a co-conspirator with John Brown, but ill health kept her from participating in the raid on Harper's Ferry. She died in 1913.

with swift, gigantic hand, sketched the vast shadows, and dashed in the high lights in which romance loves to lurk and flash forth. . . . The desperation or the magnanimity of a poor black woman has power to shake the nation that so long was deaf to her cries.

That year, Harriet Tubman was in South Carolina with a Union raiding party that rescued eight hundred slaves. She was likened to Joan of Arc by her memorialists. John Brown, who sought her advice, called her "the most of a man naturally that I ever met with." The opera, however, deals not with Harriet Tubman's Civil War exploits but with the earlier years when, an escaped slave, she returned again and again to Maryland to guide other slaves along the Underground Railroad to freedom. For those deeds she was (as a memorial tablet in Auburn, New York, where she settled, records) "called the Moses of her people." She had escaped to Philadelphia herself, but after the passing of the Fugitive Slave Law she had to take her charges to Canada before they were safe.

The opera's final chorus runs:

We will fight
So no one is a slave,
So all can live in together
In peace,
In harmony
And in freedom.

The biographies of this remarkable woman are contradictory about details and tantalizingly incomplete. She left no autobiographical narrative—such as Frederick Douglass or Sojourner

---

'I know of no one who has willingly encountered more perils and hardships to serve our enslaved people.'

—FREDERICK DOUGLASS

Truth did—but in old age delighted to recount her adventures. The passages in purported oratio recta which others set down bear out the claim of one of her biographers that "she had a highly developed sense of the dramatic, a sense of the comic, and . . . the surge and sway of the majestic rhythm of the King James version of the Bible was an integral part of her speech." Of Robert Gould Shaw's attack, with his black regiment, on Fort Wagner, she said:

> And then we saw the lightning, and that was the guns; and then we heard the rain falling, and that was the drops of blood falling; and when we came to get the crops, it was dead men that we reaped.

And of the day she crossed the state line into Pennsylvania:

> I looked at my hands to see if I was the same person now I was free. There was such a glory over everything, the sun came like gold through the trees, and over the fields, and I felt like I was in Heaven. I was free; but there was no one to welcome me to the land of freedom. I was a stranger in a strange land, and my home after all was down in the old cabin quarter with the old folks, and my brothers and sisters. But to this solemn resolution I came: I was free, and they should be free also. I would make a home for them in the North and, the Lord helping me, I would bring them all here.

In youth, she suffered a head injury—an incensed overseer flung a heavy weight at her—and throughout her life she was subject to sudden bouts of trancelike sleep. She told Thomas Garrett, the Wilmington Quaker, that she talked daily with God, and He with her. She had mysterious premonitions of impending danger and to them ascribed her ability to avoid it. Gerry Smith, the

'There was one of two things I had the right to: liberty or death. If I could not have one, I'd have the other, for no man should take me alive.'

—HARRIET TUBMAN

millionaire abolitionist, wrote that he listened often to Harriet Tubman with delight, "and I am convinced that she is not only truthful but that she has a rare discernment, and a deep and sublime philanthropy." References to her in letters and memoirs are numerous but brief. The chronicles are scrappy, and the personality of the woman, I find, remains elusive.

> We stand by the river
> If the water is deep we will swim. . . .
> We will stand on the other side.
> We have learned to march so well
> that we cannot drown.

There was an incident in Harriet Tubman's life when, warned by an inner prompting, she saved her party from capture by leading it through a swift, deep, apparently impassible stream. In the metaphors of art, as in life, rivers play a double role. Their flow, an everlasting stream, is an emblem of time, of immanence against eternity. But they are also boundaries marking stages in life's journey—for Caesar, for Alice, for Pilgrim. Harriet Tubman used to dream of flying over fields and towns, rivers and mountains, until she reached a last river over which she would try to fly: "But it appeared I wouldn't have the strength, and just as I was sinking down, there would be ladies all dressed in white over there, and they would put out their arms and pull me across."

In a program note Musgrave set out "some of the reasons why I, a white woman of Scottish descent, felt moved to write about Harriet Tubman:" the subject embodies Lincoln's "eternal struggle between two principles;" Harriet Tubman inspires an

'The wily and fearless Tubman carried a pistol on her freedom raids and if a slave had second thoughts about escaping she pulled a gun and said: "You'll be free or die!"'

—COMMONWEALTH MAGAZINE

answer to the question: "But what can one person do?" And:

> There is another overriding reason why composers are drawn to sub-
> jects that cross political and temporal boundaries and venture into
> different, often exotic settings for their works. . . . Most composers
> want to underline and emphasize the eternal nature of human
> conflicts and emotions which transcend time and place. . . .
> Harriet is every woman who dared to defy injustice and
> tyranny; she is Joan of Arc, she is Susan B. Anthony, she is
> Anne Frank, she is Mother Teresa.

'Children if you are tired, keep going. If you are hungry, keep going. If you want to taste freedom, keep going.'

—HARRIET TUBMAN

fidel castro

by Gabriel García Márquez

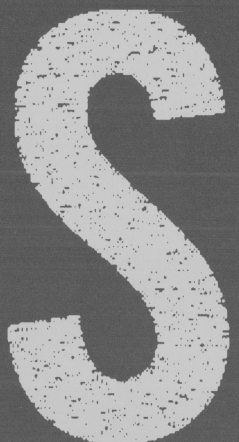

PEAKING OF A FOREIGN VISITOR whom he had accompanied for a week on a tour around Cuba, Fidel Castro said: "How that man can talk—he talks even more than I do!" It is enough to know Fidel Castro just a little to realize this was an exaggeration, a great exaggeration, because it is impossible to find anyone more addicted than he to the habit of conversation.

His devotion to the word is almost magical. At the beginning of the revolution, hardly a week after his triumphal entry into Havana, he spoke on television for seven hours without respite. It must be a world record. During the first few hours, the people of Havana, not yet familiar with the hypnotic power of that voice, sat down to listen in the traditional way. But as time passed, they went back to their daily routine, with one ear to their affairs and the other to the speech.

Fidel Castro, the son of a Cuban sugar-cane plantation owner unsuccessfully attempted to overthrow General Fulgencio Batista's government on July 26, 1953, resulting in two years in prison. Upon his release, Castro went to Mexico to plan an invasion of Cuba, and on December 2, 1956, he began the guerilla war campaign that eventually toppled Batista's government. He has been the Communist president and premier of Cuba since 1959.

"An extraordinary man. He has confronted and solved the most impossible problems. He has an unshakable faith.'

—CHE GUEVARA

Two things caught the attention of those of us hearing Fidel Castro for the first time. One was his terrible power to seduce his listeners; the other was the fragility of his voice. It was a hoarse voice, which at times was reduced to a breathless whisper. A doctor, on hearing the hoarseness, concluded that even without the marathon speeches that seemed to flow as long as the River Amazon, Fidel Castro was doomed to lose his voice within five years. Shortly afterwards, in August 1962, this prognosis seemed to have its first alarming confirmation when he was left mute after having made a speech announcing the nationalization of U.S. companies. But it was a transitory set-back which did not recur. Twenty-six years have passed since then. Fidel Castro has just turned 61, and his voice sounds just as uncertain as ever; but it continues to be his most useful and irresistible instrument in the subtle craft of the spoken word. . . .

A long time ago he said: "As important as learning to work is learning to rest." But his methods of rest seem too original, and apparently do not exclude conversation. Once he left an intense work session close to midnight, with visible signs of exhaustion, and returned in the pre-dawn hours fully recovered after swimming for a couple of hours. Private parties run counter to his character, as he is one of the rare Cubans who neither sings nor dances, and the very few he does attend change in nature the moment he arrives. Perhaps he does not realize. Perhaps he is not aware of the power his presence imposes, a presence which immediately seems to fill all the space, although he is neither as tall nor as corpulent as he appears at first glance. I have seen the most self-assured people lose their poise in his company, by contriving to look composed or adopting an exaggerated air of confidence, without ever imagining that he is as intimidated as they are, and has to make the initial effort so that it is not noticed. I have always believed that the plural which he often uses when speaking of his own acts is not so majestic as it seems, but rather a poetic license to conceal his shyness.

Inevitably the dancing is interrupted, the music stops, the dinner is put off, and the crowd gathers around him to join in the conversation which begins immediately. He can remain like that for any length of time, standing up, without drinking or eating anything. Sometimes, before going to bed, he will knock very late at the door of a close friend, where he can show up unannounced, and says he's staying only five minutes. He says it with such sincerity that he does not even take a seat. Little by little, he gets stimulated again by the new conversation, and after a while he collapses into an easy chair and stretches out his legs, saying: "I feel like a new man." That is how it is: weary of talking, he rests by talking. . . .

This could explain his absolute confidence in direct contact. Even the most difficult speeches seem like casual talks, like those he held with students in the courtyards of the university at the outset of the revolution. In fact, and especially outside Havana, it is not unusual for someone to call out to him from the crowd at a public meeting and a shouted dialogue will begin. He has a language for every occasion and a different form of persuasion depending on his different interlocutors, be they workers, farmers, students, scientists, politicians, writers or foreign visitors. He can reach each one at their own level with vast and varied information that allows him to move easily in any medium. But his personality is so complex and unpredictable that any one of them can form a different impression of him in the same encounter.

One thing is certain: wherever he may be, however and with whomever, Fidel Castro is there to win. I do not think anyone in this world could be a worse loser. His attitude in the face of defeat, even in the slightest events of daily life, seems to obey a private logic: he will not even admit it, and he does not have a moment's peace until he manages to invert the terms and turn it into a victory. But whatever it may be, and wherever, everything happens within the ambit of an inexhaustible conversation.

The subject can be anything, according to the interest of the audience,

> 'I am inspired by the grand spectacle of the great revolutions of history, because they have always signified the triumph of aims embodying the welfare and happiness of the vast majority.'
>
> —FIDEL CASTRO

'Don't take me
as a role model....
I have tried to
be a good revolu-
tionary. I have
tried to be a
good soldier.'

—FIDEL CASTRO

but often the opposite occurs when it is he who takes a single subject to all his audiences. This tends to happen during the periods in which he is exploring an idea which is bothering him, and no once can be more obsessive than he when he has set out to get to the bottom of something. There is no project, however grandiose or minute, which he does not undertake with a fierce passion, especially if he is facing adversity. Never than at such times does he look better, appear in a better mood or in higher spirits. Someone who believes he knows him once commented: "Things must be going very badly, because you look radiant."

Another vital source of information, of course, is books. Perhaps the aspect of Fidel Castro's personality least in keeping with the image created by his adversaries is that of being a voracious reader. No one can explain how he finds the time or what methods he uses to read so much and so quickly, although he insists that there is nothing special about it. In his cars, from the prehistoric Oldsmobile to successive Soviet Zils, up to the current Mercedes, there has always been a light for reading at night. Many times he has taken a book in the pre-dawn hours, and commented on it the following morning. He reads English, but does not speak it. In any case he prefers to read in Spanish, and at any hour is ready to read any piece of paper with letters on it that may fall into his hands. When he needs some very recent book, which has not yet been translated, he has it translated. A doctor friend sent him, as a courtesy, his treatise on orthopedics which had just been published without, of course, any pretension that he read it, but a week later he received a letter from him with a long list of observations. He is an habitual reader of economic and historical subjects. When he read the memoirs of Lee Iacocca, he discovered several such incredible errors that he sent to New York for the English version, to compare it with the Spanish. Indeed, the translator had once again confused the meaning of the word billion in the two languages. He is a good reader of literature and follows it closely. I have on my conscience having initiated him in the addiction of quick-consumption best-sellers and then keeping him up to date as an antidote to official documents.

Still, his immediate and most fruitful source of information continues to be conversation. He has the habit of quick interrogations, which resemble a *matriushka*, the Russian doll from whose interior a similar, smaller one emerges, then another, until the smallest one possible is left. He asks successive questions in instantaneous bursts until he discovers the why of the why of the final why. It is difficult for his interlocutor not to feel subjected to an inquisitorial examination.

Many times I have seen him arrive at my house very late at night, still trailing the last scraps of a limitless day. Many times I have asked him how things were going, and more than once he answered me: "Very well, we have all the reservoirs full." I have seen him open the refrigerator to eat a piece of cheese, which was perhaps the first thing he had eaten since breakfast. I have seen him telephone a friend in Mexico to ask her for the recipe for a dish he had liked, and I have seen him copy it down leaning against the counter, among the still unwashed pots and pans from dinner, while someone on television sang an ancient song: "Life is an Express Train That Travels Thousands of Leagues." I have heard him in his few moments of nostalgia evoking the pastoral dawns of his rural childhood, the sweetheart of his youth who left, the things he could have done differently to win from life. One night, while he was eating vanilla ice-cream in slow little spoonfuls, I saw him so overwhelmed by the weight of the destinies of so many people, so removed from himself, that for an instant he seemed different to me from the man he had always been. Then I asked him what he would most like to do in this world, and he answered immediately: "Just hang around on some street corner."

'One thing is certain: wherever he may be, Fidel Castro is there to win. I do not think anyone in this world could be a worse loser.... He does not have a moment's peace until he manages to turn it into a victory'

—GABRIEL GARCIA MARQUEZ

salvador allende

by Ariel Dorfman

O N THE NIGHT OF SEPTEMBER 11, 1973, WHEN General Augusto Pinochet ordered the body of Salvador Allende to be secretly buried in a grave by the sea, he could not have imagined that the very President he had just overthrown and whose legacy he was confident of extirpating forever from the memory of Chile would someday be given a tumultuous second funeral, in which many of the very people who had contributed to his downfall would honor him. It took Pinochet only a few hours to be rid of the man he had betrayed. It would take the Chilean people, on the other hand, seventeen years of resistance to rescue Salvador Allende from the anonymous earth to which he had been banished, because in order to do so, first they would have to accomplish the more dangerous task of rescuing the democracy their President had died to defend.

Salvador Allende, born in Valparaíso, Chile, in 1908, was a founding member of the Chilean Socialist Party. He served as president of Chile from 1970-73, when, after his government won by popular election, it was overthrown by a military junta led by General Augusto Pinochet and Allende was killed.

'Never had brute force come up against such resistance, carried out in the military field by a man of ideas, whose weapons were always the spoken and written word.'

—FIDEL CASTRO

On March 11 of [1990], as soon as Patricio Aylwin, Chile's new democratic President, entered La Moneda, the presidential palace where Allende had died, plans for a public farewell and burial were started. Aylwin's first visitor was, in fact, Allende's widow, Tencha—and his first words of greeting to her were, "I owe Salvador a funeral." And he kept his promise: The man who, as president of the Christian Democratic Party in 1973, had led the opposition to Allende; who had refused to sign an agreement with him that might have avoided the coup; who had gone to the military a few days after the takeover to congratulate them and suggest, fruitlessly and ingenuously as it turned out, that they hand power over to the waiting civilians, would be the main speaker at Allende's funeral.

Most Chileans expected the family to choose September 11 as the date for that funeral, the anniversary, after all, of Allende's death—a fitting way, they thought, of closing and completing a circle that had been broken. But Allende's kin showed a deeper wisdom and chose September 4 instead, the day when we Chileans have, for most of our independent history, held our presidential balloting. It was on that date, exactly twenty years before, that Allende had become the first socialist in history to come to power in democratic elections, opening up the breathtaking possibility that deep structural change could be achieved through peaceful means, that socialism could be built without repressing its adversaries. To hold the ceremony that day was to reaffirm Allende's democratic credentials and therefore to deny the legitimacy of the military intervention—which had been contrived, carried out and then justified by Chile's conservative forces, with the enthusiastic aid of Nixon, Kissinger and company, as the only way of saving the country from "communism." All the horrors that were to follow could henceforth be trumpeted as the lesser of two evils, authoritarianism as the unfortunate remedy to stem the tide of totalitarianism—as long, of course, as Allende could be painted as a Marxist autocrat.

Allende's public rehabilitation, the fact that a socialist should be honored officially as a great democrat precisely at a moment in contemporary history when socialism is in crisis because of its failure to be pluralistic and participatory, drove Chilean right wingers and assorted army generals into a veritable frenzy. In a barrage of ludicrous statements over the past months they have accused the Allendistas of wanting, with the acquiescence of the Christian Democrats, to "rewrite history"—as if history belonged only to the people in power and as if they themselves had not spent the past seventeen years rewriting it with bullets and censorship; as if the people of Chile had not been writing and rewriting Allende's story and our own story all these years, writing it through our protests, rewriting it in the silence of our hearts, biding our time until we would be strong enough to resurrect into daylight the body we had kept alive in the forbidden darkness of our imagination.

On the day of the funeral, watching the calm, fervent crowds, the photographs hidden inside mattresses all these years and finally held aloft as the coffin went by, the old man crying like a baby right into a Chilean flag crumpled in his hands, the youngsters who had not been born when Allende disappeared calling out his name like an incantation against death, the thousands upon thousands of the dirt poor who lost a day's pay so they would be able to tell their grandchildren that they had been here, the women in wheelchairs pushing themselves toward Allende's new grave as if it were heaven, the flowers falling from a myriad of hands, I wondered at the miracle of it all, at how these people had kept Allende's memory burning in the midst of their despair and terror. I wondered at the millions of hours they must have waited for this day, while the soldiers ravaged their land and their families. Allende had survived because these people had survived.

It had been exactly seventeen years since his supporters had last seen Salvador Allende alive. I had been among the million shouting

'You must never forget that, sooner rather than later, the grand avenues will be opened and free men will march on to build a better society.'

—SALVADOR ALLENDE

marchers who had poured into the streets of Santiago on September 4, 1973, to celebrate the third anniversary of our electoral victory. That night it had taken the group I had joined seven fervorous hours to reach the balcony of La Moneda, where Allende was saluting the multitudes. We marched by, singing and chanting and unfurling flags, and for a magic moment as we passed our leader we somehow convinced ourselves that we were as strong as ever, that we could still change the history of humanity and free our country from the misery that had plagued it ever since we could remember. Then we looked back and saw him there, standing alone on that balcony waving a distant white handkerchief, and something unspoken and grievous inside every one of us made us turn the corner and go around the block and mingle with the next overflowing column and pass by again one long last time. Our hoarse voices might roar that the people united would never be defeated, that we would overcome, Venceremos, over and over, but what we were really doing that night was saying goodbye to our President. We must have known deep inside that Allende's days were numbered, that all our days were numbered and that those who were doing the numbering and would soon do the killing were the military.

All of a sudden, in the midst of the clenched fists and chanted slogans of the immense crowd, I had the dizzying sensation that time had stopped, that our goodbye at La Moneda and our goodbye at this cemetery so many years later were consecutive, that nothing had happened in between.

The illusion soon dissipated.

Time had indeed passed, in Chile and in the world. Not all was victory that day. If Pinochet had been unable to block Allende's funeral, Allende's followers had been unable to oust Pinochet totally from power. It is not merely the fact that the general is still Commander in Chief of the army; that his designated cronies hold veto power in the Senate, in the

'The Chilean revolution leaves a vision of the government that fought for the people and socialism, of the great revolutionary president who never buckled.'

—EDWARD BOORSTEIN

Supreme Court and in the townships, obstructing popular sovereignty; it is not only that mistrust and lies have damaged Chile's moral landscape and will affect who knows how many future generations but that Pinochet's policies have altered the way in which Chile dreams of itself and its future.

The tragedy is that, like that other experiment of those years that attempted to reconcile socialism with democracy, the Prague Spring of 1968, we never got the chance to explore an alternative. We were crushed, respectively, by the self-proclaimed world representatives of socialism and of democracy, trapped by the fears of the cold war. In the Chilean case, even though Allende had personally condemned the Soviet invasion of Czechoslovakia, he did not, and possibly could not, as I could not and did not along with most of the left, draw the deeper conclusions of that failure. We did not see the Eastern European search as a mirror in which to learn. We were so much more democratic than our right-wing enemies that we thought it unnecessary to look deep into our own ambiguities and weaknesses.

To critique those ideas, and many others, is to dare to begin a real conversation with Allende. Finally, that may be the most far-reaching consequence of the September 4 funeral. While Allende lay in an unmarked tomb, denied to us as the desaparecidos of Chile are still denied to their relatives by the armed forces, we had to keep his myth alive—and one can receive consolation or inspiration from a myth but one cannot hold a dialogue with the man behind it.

Now that Salvador Allende, so dead and so alive, has been returned to the earth we set aside for him all these years, we can begin to live with him and without him, in a world that needs more than ever the social justice and the full participation he dreamt of for all.

'He died with unwavering confidence in the strength of the people, fully aware he defended with his life the cause of the workers and of the poor.'

—BEATRIZ ALLENDE BUSSI

lech walesa

by Neal Ascherson

ECH WALESA, AN ELECTRICIAN, became for sixteen months one of the most famous men in the world. He
led the strike which began at the Lenin shipyard in Gdansk
on 14 August 1980. He signed the Gdansk agreement on
31 August which announced the triumph of the strike and
the emergence of the "independent, self-managing trade
union Solidarity," and as the union spread throughout
Poland, eventually acquiring some nine and a half million
members, there was no question that anyone but Walesa
should be the first chairman of its provisional executive.
The union's first national congress in September and
October the following year re-elected him chairman, against
the candidature of several more militant rivals, and he was
still Solidarity's leader on 13 December 1981, when
General Wojciech Jaruzelski imposed martial law, sus-

Lech Walesa, born in Poland in 1943, was a shipyard worker in Gdansk
who became a leader of Solidarity, the independent trade union, openly
questioning the policies of both church and state in Poland, and was
imprisoned for a year as a result. He won the Nobel Peace Prize in 1983
and a landslide victory in his bid for the Polish presidency in 1990. He
was president until 1995.

pended Solidarity and arrested thousands of its officials and activists. Walesa's face, during those months, appeared on magazine covers and television screens in every country. The teleprinters relayed across the globe every comment he cared to make. Young men in France and Germany, the United States and Britain, grew imitations of his long "Sarmatian" moustache. Next to the Pope, he was the most celebrated Pole alive.

I forget exactly when I first saw him. It was during the August strike at Gdansk, when we in the world press had only just learned to spell his name. The negotiations with the government were nearing their climax. Perhaps I first saw him in one of those sudden eddies of the crowd, as he tore across the shipyard scribbling autographs and scattering little colored cards of the Madonna of Czestochowa. It was hard to get a proper look; he seemed always to rush, never to walk, and the press of men in drab overalls around him constantly hid his short figure from view. My first chance to study him properly came during a break in the talks, a few days later. The door of the strike presidium room had been left unguarded, and I strolled in. Walesa was sitting on a chair, with a little girl in a cheap tartan dress on his knee (one of his many children), talking to a group of his advisers. They were standing, frowning down at him, raising difficulties. As he glanced up at them, I was struck by the foxiness of his appearance: the long narrow nose, the sharp russet eyes, the sense of quickness and cunning which this look and his staccato sentences put across.

As the strike went on, the nature of his hold over the movement turned out to be more complicated than it had at first seemed. Walesa was at once more and less than a demagogue. He was a consummate, even outrageous manipulator; I once saw him put three mutually exclusive resolutions to the main strike committee within a few minutes and have them all accepted by acclaim. He could be dictatorial, often snatching the microphone from a colleague who was in mid-sentence. He was certainly a born

'[Walesa's Nobel prize] is a victory for those who seek to enlarge the human spirit over those who seek to crush it.'

—RONALD REAGAN

trouble-maker, but a trouble-maker who lusted after compromise rather than extremes. As his whole career in those sixteen months showed, Walesa adored the actual business of negotiating: the shatteringly hard opening position, the leaving of doors ajar, the gradual trading-off in hard talk sessions until both sides could shake hands with pride on a gleaming new settlement. Many of his colleagues entirely lacked this taste. They wanted to leave the negotiating table with all their demands won and no concessions made. But Walesa preferred a genuine joint settlement, talked out until opponents had become accomplices. "*Polak z Polakiem musi się dogadac*"—"Pole must talk things out with Pole," he used endlessly to repeat.

"Charisma" is not a useful word. As Maria Janion says in this book [*Walesa*], the electrician did somehow communicate electricity, send currents circuting between him and his mass audiences. But it was the ambiguity of his relation to the crowd which struck me most at Gdansk. On the one hand the workers worshiped Walesa; they cheered him, chanted his name, brought him little presents, reached out to touch him as he passed. And yet, on the other hand, this worship was entirely provisional. They were well aware that Walesa was fallible and vain, and when he put a foot wrong they would noisily oppose him. Is it possible to combine passionate loyalty and affectionate contempt? They were combined at Gdansk. It was just because the workers saw that "Leszek" was one of them—and no better than they—that they managed to square that psychological circle.

For he really was a workers' tribune, which is more than a spell-binder. The influence of Jimmy Reid, a leader of the great workers' take-over at Upper Clyde shipyards in 1971, was as much to do with his talents as a comic as with his socialist eloquence. Walesa dominated the Gdansk strike not through oratory but by something much more proletarian: patter. He made people laugh, seemed a chancer, a card. And he conveyed the hint that he was more at home with foul means than fair. In Glasgow and

'As a revolutionary I would never want to see another revolution.'

—LECH WALESA

Gdansk, where "they" frame the Queensberry Rules so that nobody at the bottom of the heap can win by them, a touch of lawlessness in a leader is well taken.

He seemed to bask in publicity. But in reality he was evasive with journalists, almost never dropping his guard or allowing himself to enter a serious conversation (an exception that proves the rule is the interview with Marzena and Tadeusz Wozniak in this book, who lured Walesa further than he meant to go). Behind the bonhomie, he probably despised the mass media, enjoying their flattery but clever enough to give as little as he could in return. Immensely proud of his power as the workers' spokesman, Walesa never mentally crossed the line which divides workers from the Establishment. Those who gave him power could take it away again. As he says here, "I was at the bottom, and I will be at the bottom." His vanity, which was considerable, was not really personal but an expression of pride that this electrician, pious but no better than he should be, had been chosen to perform this task. Chosen by whom? Not simply by the working class. Walesa's self-confidence was messianic, and he may have taken seriously the idea that it was God and his Mother who had chosen him to lead the nation out of bondage. And like many messianic figures "called" from obscurity (Joan of Arc, Cincinnatus), he hoped to become a nobody again when his assignment was over.

The essays and tributes in this book tell us above all what Walesa meant to his fellow-Poles. They show us where he came from—the valiant little Land of Dobrzyn devastated by so many of Poland's political disasters, the locked and empty hut behind a birch brake where he was born, the cottage of the grandfather who also had whiskers and once hid Józef Pilsudski from the police. And they show how Polish literary culture effortlessly pervaded the subconscious of this man so impatient that he claims never to have finished a book. But in the end, this work is an extraordinary study in

'You must provide the world not with the fish, but with fishing rods.'

—LECH WALESA

Polish nationalism, that intense and sealed-off culture in which industrial workers are at ease with their own classic poetry, in which the time dimension dissolves so that lines of nineteenth-century heroic drama may be the best guide to twentieth-century political crises, in which the cause of independence, Catholic belief and personal morality are compressed into a single explosive compound.

There are elements of ancestor-worship here. The bloody shirt of the insurrectionary is handed down from generation to generation. The first written expression of the Gdansk strikes was—as Maria Janion tells us here—to pin a verse of Byron's to a cross, that verse which speaks of "... Freedom's battle once begun, Bequeathed by bleeding sire to son ..."

To mark their peaceful intentions, the strikers left out the word "bleeding." But those lines also hold an important clue to Walesa's own personality. The most powerful of all his motives in his years of illegal struggle before 1980 was a sort of filial piety, a vow to honor the dead of the strikes of December 1970. Year after year on 16 December he made his way to the place outside the Lenin shipyard where the monument now stands, urging his comrades to bring building stones with them, and every year the little group was dispersed or arrested only to return again on the next anniversary. This obsession with the martyred dead, so much a part of the national psychology, was the source of his driving anger and his obstinacy. This young electrician is best understood, when all has been said, as a Polish Antigone.

"Politics is changing in Poland. In the beginning of Walesa's term... institutions were less trusted. Now people are starting to put their trust in the institutions of democracy.'

—ANDRZEJ RYCHARD

john brown

by W.E.B. Du Bois

OUNG JOHN BROWN'S FIRST BROAD CONTACT with life and affairs came with the War of 1812, during which he saw shameful defeat, heard treason broached, and knew of cheating and chicanery. Disease and death left its slimy trail as it crept homeward through the town of Hudson from Detroit.

But in all these early years of the making of this man, one incident stands out as foretaste and prophecy—an incident of which we know only the indefinite outline, and yet one which unconsciously foretold to the boy the life deed of the man. It was during the war that a certain land-lord welcomed John to his home whither the boy had ridden with cattle a hundred miles through the wilderness. He praised the big grave and bashful lad to his guests and made much of him. John, however, discovered something far

---

John Brown was born in Connecticut in 1800, and worked as a tanner, land surveyor, shepherd, and farmer. A long-time abolitionist, Brown led a small group in an attack on pro-slavery men in Pottawatomie Creek, Kansas on May 24, 1856. With the hope of setting up a free slave state in Virginia, Brown and his men seized the armory at Harper's Ferry on October 16, 1859. He was captured, tried and hung for treason.

more interesting than praise and good food in the landlord's parlor, and this was another boy in the landlord's yard. Fellow souls were scarce with this backwoodsman and his diffidence warmed to the kindly welcome of the stranger, especially because he was black, half-naked and wretched. In John's very ear the kind voices of the master and his folk turned to harsh abuse with this black boy. At night the slave lay in the bitter cold and once they beat the wretched thing before John's very eyes with an iron shovel, and again and again struck him with any weapon that chanced. In wide-eyed silence John looked on and questioned, Was the boy bad or stupid? No, he was active, intelligent and with the great warm sympathy of his race did the stranger "numerous little acts of kindness," so that John readily, in his straightforward candor, acknowledged him "fully if not more than his equal." That the black worked and worked hard and steadily was in John's eyes no hardship—rather a pleasure. Was not the world work? But that this boy was fatherless and motherless, and that all slaves must of necessity be fatherless and motherless with none to protect them or provide for them, save at the will or caprice of the master—this was to the half-grown man a thing of fearful portent and he asked, "Is God their Father?" And what he asked, a million and a half black bondmen were asking through the land. . . .

In 1839, a Negro preacher named Fayette was visiting Brown, and bringing his story of persecution and injustice. Solemnly John Brown arose; he was then a man of nearly forty years, tall, dark and clean-shaven; by him sat his young wife of twenty-two and his oldest boys of eighteen, sixteen and fifteen. Six other children slept in the room back of the dark preacher. John Brown told them of his purpose to make active war on slavery, and bound his family in solemn and secret compact to labor for emancipation. And then, instead of standing to pray, as was his wont, he fell upon his knees and implored God's blessing on his enterprise.

'John Brown, bearded like an Old Testament Prophet, led an army of five black men and thirteen white men into the village of Harper's Ferry... to destroy slavery.'

—KEN BURNS

This marks a turning-point in John Brown's life: in his boyhood he had disliked slavery and his antipathy toward it grew with his years; yet of necessity it occupied but little of a life busy with breadwinning. Gradually, however, he saw the gathering of the mighty struggle about him; the news of the skirmish battles of the greatest moral war of the century aroused and quickened him, and all the more when they struck the tender chords of his acquaintanceships and sympathies. He saw his friends hurt and imposed on until at last, gradually, then suddenly, it dawned upon him that he must fight this monster slavery. He did not now plan physical warfare—he was yet a non-resistant, hating war, and did not dream of Harper's Ferry; but he set his face toward the goal and whithersoever the Lord led, he was ready to follow. He still, too, had his living to earn—his family to care for. Slavery was not yet the sole object of his life, but as he passed on in his daily duties he was determined to seize every opportunity to strike it a blow.

Halfway between Maine and Florida, in the heart of the Alleghanies, a mighty gateway lifts its head and discloses a scene which, a century and a quarter ago, Thomas Jefferson said was "worth a voyage across the Atlantic." He continues: "You stand on a very high point of land; on your right comes up the Shenandoah, having ranged along the foot of the mountain a hundred miles to find a vent; on your left approaches the Potomac, in quest of a passage also. In the moment of their junction they rush together against the mountain, rend it asunder, and pass off to the sea."

This is Harper's Ferry and this was the point which John Brown chose for his attack on American slavery. He chose Harper's Ferry because a United States arsenal was there and the capture of this would give that dramatic climax to the inception of his plan which was so necessary to its success. But that was a minor reasons. The foremost and decisive reason was that Harper's Ferry was the safest natural entrance to the Great Black Way, an area where there was massed in 1859 at least three of the four million slaves.

> **'John Brown's plan was the attempt of a fanatic or madman and could only end in failure.'**
>
> **—ROBERT E.**

'I am quite certain that the crimes of this guilty land will never be purged away but with blood. I had, as I now think vainly, flattered myself that without very much bloodshed it might be done.'

—JOHN BROWN

[But there was a] fatal hitch. The farm was not over three miles from the schoolhouse, and there was a heavy farm-wagon with four large strong horses and a dozen men or more to help. The fact that it took these men eleven hours to move two wagon-loads of material less than three miles is the secret of the extraordinary failure of Brown's foray at a time when victory was in his grasp.

Robert E. Lee, with 100 marines, arrived just before midnight on Monday and one of the prisoners tells the story of the last stand:

"When Colonel Lee came with the government troops in the night, he at once sent a flag of truce by his aid, J. E. B. Stuart, to notify Brown of his arrival, and in the name of the United States to demand his surrender, advising him to throw himself on the clemency of the government. Brown declined to accept Colonel Lee's terms, and determined to await the attack."

Thus John Brown's raid ended. Seven of the men—[including] John Brown himself—were captured and hanged.

At high noon on Tuesday, October 18th, the raid was over. John Brown lay wounded and blood-stained on the floor and the governor of Virginia bent over him.

"Who are you?" he asked.

"My name is John Brown; I have been well known as old John Brown of Kansas. Two of my sons were killed here today, and I'm dying too. I came here to liberate slaves, and was to receive no reward. I have acted from a sense of duty, and am content to await my fate; but I think the crowd have treated me badly. I am an old man. Yesterday I could have killed whom I chose; but I had no desire to kill any person, and would not have killed a man had they not tried to kill me and my men. I could have sacked and burned the town, but did not; I have treated the persons whom I took as hostages kindly, and I appeal to them for the truth of what I say. If I had succeeded in running off slaves this time, I could have raised twenty times as many men as I have now, for a similar expedition. But I have failed."

The day of his dying, December 2, dawned glorious; twenty-four hours before he had kissed his wife good-bye, and on this morning he visited his doomed companions. At last he turned toward the place of his hanging. Since early morning three thousand soldiers had been marching and counter-marching around the scaffold, which had been erected a half mile from Charlestown, encircling it for fifteen miles; a hush sat on the hearts of men. John Brown rode out into the morning. "This is a beautiful land," he said. It was beautiful. Wide, glistening, rolling fields flickered in the sunlight. Beyond, the Shenandoah went rolling northward, and still afar rose the mighty masses of the Blue Ridge, where Nat Turner had fought and died, where Gabriel had looked for refuge and where John Brown had builded his awful dream. Some say he kissed a Negro child as he passed, but Andrew Hunter vehemently denies it. "No Negro could get access to him," he says, and he is probably right; and yet all about him as he hung there knelt the funeral guard he prayed for when he said:

"My love to all who love their neighbors. I have asked to be spared from having any weak or hypocritical prayers made over me when I am publicly murdered, and that my only religious attendants be poor little dirty, ragged, bare-headed, and barefooted slave boys and girls, led by some gray-headed slave mother. Farewell! Farewell!"

'You may dispose of me very easily... but this question is still to be settled—this Negro question, I mean. The end of that is not yet.'

—JOHN BROWN

subcomandante marcos

by Alma Guillermoprieto

O N THE EVENING OF FEBRUARY 9TH, at a press conference in Mexico City that had been announced less than two hours before, an aide to the Attorney General played a strange game of peekaboo with photographers and a crowd of sweating, jostling reporters. In his right hand the aide held an oversized black-and white slide of a ski mask and a pair of large, dark eyes, and in his left a black-and-white photograph of a Milquetoasty-looking young man with a beard and large, dark eyes. After we were allowed to study the two for a few seconds, the aid slipped the slide over the photograph. Voilà! Subcomandante Marcos, the dashing leader of an Indian peasant revolt in southeastern Mexico, the hero of a thousand fervent letters addressed to the Mexican nation, the postmodern revolutionary who has contributed mightily to what in this turbulent year,

Subcomandante Marcos, the leader of the Zapatistas in Chiapas, Mexico, wears a mask—until recently no one knew his true identity. Still, very little is known about this guerilla warrior and philosopher, Marxist, actor, poet, writer, and member of the Front for National Liberation. But his masked visage and excellent manipulations of public perceptions of his Movement have made him into a revolutionary icon.

with its hemorrhaging economy and political murder scandals, looks like the steady crumbling of a sixty-six-year-old regime—this masked idol is Clark Kent. His name, the Attorney General announced, is Rafael Sebastián Guillén, and he is a philosophy graduate and former university professor. The aide continued imposing the slide of Marcos on the photograph of Guillén and flipping them apart again—now we saw him, now we didn't—until the storm of camera flashes subsided, and then we left.

The revelation of Marcos's identity was part of a two-pronged strategy by President Ernesto Zedillo Ponce de León to break the stalemate that has existed in the state of Chiapas since the Ejército Zapatista de Liberación Nacional, or E.Z.L.N.—a ragtag army of Mayan peasants lead by Subcomandante Marcos—rose up in revolt there, on January 1, 1994. Even as we watched the slide show, Army troops were preparing to move into the mountainous and overwhelmingly rural southeastern part of Chiapas—almost on the border with Guatemala—where the Zapatistas had maintained their unofficially recognized *territorio liberada* for thirteen months. Villages were being retaken without a fight, and their inhabitants, including the Zapatista fighters among them, were fleeing into the ravines and jungle-covered mountains. President Zedillo said that the Army was going into the area only to provide backing for the federal agents who would attempt to serve Marcos with an arrest warrant, but this was a transparent excuse, for thousands of troops swarmed in, and have continued to take positions farther and farther inside the territory.

Before the offensive began, the stalemate between the Zapatistas and the government had lasted so long that it seemed permanent. All actual fighting ended barely twelve days after the New Year's Day rebellion got under way last year, in the lovely town of San Cristóbal de las Casas. The peasant army had vowed in its declaration of war that it would march to Mexico City and overthrow the government of President Carlos Salinas de

'We say enough is enough! We are the descendants of those who built this nation, we are millions of dispossessed, and we call upon all our brethren to join our crusade, the only option to avoid dying of starvation!'

—SUBCOMANDANTE MARCOS

Gortari, but, instead, it suffered significant losses and scored no military victories. It did, however, capture Mexicans' imagination: televised interviews of Mayan peasants in makeshift uniforms, who said that they were fighting not only for a change in their own desperate circumstances but to rid the nation of a corrupt and slothful regime, brought thousands of demonstrators out into the streets all over Mexico during the first days of January, demanding an end to what threatened to turn into an Army slaughter of the armed Zapatistas and their families.

Faced with the politically volatile option of turning the Army against its own people, Salinas, on January 12th, called for a ceasefire. Thereafter, and through the transfer of power in December from Salinas to Ernesto Zedillo, following the Presidential elections last August, talks and attempts at talks promoted by both sides led to no fruitful agreement, but they at least kept the ceasefire from breaking down. Even in December, when the Zapatistas pushed beyond their control zone to protest the stalemate and what they saw as massive fraud in the elections for governor of Chiapas, the rebels and the government troops managed to come within a few hundred feet of each other without a shot being fired.

The Army's offensive certainly appears to have taken Marcos completely by surprise. Much of the anxious speculation about what will happen next in Chiapas centers on his personality and his aims—on what he believes in and to what lengths he is willing to take the war. Will he negotiate to keep his peasant troops from suffering further? Does he really want nothing less than the overthrow of the government? And is he in fact the man in the photograph?

As far as I could tell on the night of the Attorney General's press conference, as I tried to make the ten-year-old I.D. shot of a bland Rafael Guillén jibe with my recollection of the masked man I had talked with last April, the ski-masked slide we were being shown could have been slipped

'Marcos has always maintained that he is only the voice of the people, not their leader or guide.'

—CONSEJO GUERRENSE

'We are engaged in a struggle of memory against oblivion; the market buys our past and present and runs it through the shredder to make way for industrial parks and commercial space.'

—SUBCOMANDANTE MARCOS

just as persuasively over a photograph of Richard Nixon. The Marcos whom I and other journalists interviewed in the Zapatista control zone was a mesmerizing personality—self-possessed, considerate, ironic, and theatrical. He liked to make journalists spend hours, or days, waiting for him, and then he would appear in the dead of night and talk endlessly, puffing on a pipe, tugging at the uncomfortable ski mask, and asking as many questions as he answered—uncannily well informed about the intellectual and media world beyond Chiapas. When I said that it was delusionary to think that the Zapatistas could really take Mexico City, he answered, "Weren't we there already by January 2nd? We were everywhere, on the lips of everyone—in the subway, on the radio. And our flag was in the Zócalo"—the central plaza.

While the resemblance between Guillén's eyes and Marcos's—the only part of his physiognomy we are all acquainted with—is not conclusive (Marcos's are a hazel-brown, for one and the photograph is black-and-white), the account of the E.Z.L.N.'s history and Marcos's role in it which the Attorney General's office has been leaking to the press does coincide with much that has been said privately about Marcos in Chiapas for some time.

There was a very real sense in which, during the past thirteen months, Marcos fought the Zapatista war single-handed. It was, after all, a public-relations war, and the Indian fighters—most of whom spoke little Spanish, and for whom the government had provided, at most, a few years of elementary schooling—were not equipped for the sophisticated exchanges with the government and the Mexican public which such a war required. It was Marcos who wrote the letters, and also the communiqués signed by something called the Clandestine Indigenous Revolutionary Committee—General Command, which is supposedly the highest authority within the E.Z.L.N. (It is more likely the body, consisting of village authorities, that makes the real decisions affecting daily life in the Zapatista zone, while Marcos himself seems to have decisive influence, if not absolute power, in questions having to do with war and relations with the central government.) It was Marcos who granted the vast majority of the interviews—or, at least, the ones that got quoted. It was he who drew up the list of accredited "war correspondents," and signed our laminated mint-green credentials. It was he who stage-managed the moving E.Z.L.N. events at which glamorous visitors from Mexico City and abroad watched Indian peasants parade in homemade uniforms, carrying hunting rifles and other guns and—in the absence of real weapons—carved wood imitations of guns. And it was his adroit manipulation of this array of symbolic weapons that mobilized public opinion in favor of the E.Z.L.N. and kept the war the Zapatistas had invited at bay.

Marcos, however, cannot fight a real war by himself, and, on the basis of the Army's stunning advance over the last three weeks, it seems that any attempt by the E.Z.L.N. troops to take on the Mexican Army can only end in tragedy. The total number of dead that reporters have reliably been able to come up with for the offensive is fewer than ten, and this is because, rather than fight, the Zapatistas and their families fled by the thousand into the jungly, ravine-crossed mountains that stand between their homes, in the former control zone, and what remains of the Lacandón jungle.

There was a phrase one heard everywhere, stated sometimes fear-fully, sometimes with joy: "*Los indios perdieron el miedo*"— "The Indians are no longer afraid." Made fearless by the armed Zapatistas, los indios invaded some two thousand cattle ranches and coffee farms. The owners are threat-ening to take up arms in defense of their land. Los indios also did fierce, bloody battle with each other over issues of religion and politics, which always had their roots in land disputes.

'We will abide by all we have written in our heart and in our word. Everything for everybody; nothing for ourselves!'

—SUBCOMANDANTE MARCOS

elie wiesel

by Stefan Kanfer

N 1944, A 15-YEAR-OLD BOY WAS TAKEN from his house in Sighet, Hungary, and sent to a Nazi death camp. [In the spring of 1985] President Reagan presented him with a gold medal at the White House "in recognition of his humanitarian efforts and outstanding contributions to world literature and human rights."

There can be no longer journey than the one Elie Wiesel has taken from a cell in Auschwitz to the corridors of Washington. "How can you measure it?" he asks. "In the suffering of a people? In the recesses of history?" The questions are rhetorical. No gauge exists; no one has ever made the trip before. The voyage is charted in three words inscribed on his medal: AUTHOR, TEACHER, WITNESS.

The witness was born in the charred world of the Holocaust. "Never shall I forget that night, the first night

Elie Wiesel was born 1928 in Sighet, Romania. He survived his internment at Birkenau, Auschwitz, Buna, and Buchenwald concentration camps, though his parents and one sister did not. The first of the many books this Nobel Prize winning author would write about his experiences, <u>Night</u>, was published in the mid-1950s. He has written prolifically since then.

in camp, which has turned my life into one long night," he recalls in his first book. "Never shall I forget that smoke. Never shall I forget the little faces of the children, whose bodies I saw turned into wreaths of smoke beneath a silent blue sky."

As World War II came to a close, the gaunt and dolorous child was liberated at yet another death camp, Buchenwald. His parents and a sister had been murdered. How had he survived two of the most notorious killing fields of the century? "I will never know," he says. "I was always weak. I never ate. The slightest wind would turn me over. In Buchenwald they sent 10,000 to their deaths each day. I was always in the last hundred near the gate. They stopped. Why?"

The inquiry was a burden as ineradicable as the number, A-7713, tattooed on his arm by a German official. "So heavy was my anguish," he remembers, "that in the spring of 1945 I made a vow: not to speak, not to touch upon the essential for at least ten years. Long enough to unite the language of humanity with the silence of the dead."

The boy refused repatriation and found his way to France, where he worked as a choir director, translator and, eventually, journalist. It was during an interview in 1954 with Roman Catholic novelist Francois Mauriac that literature took an abrupt turn.

"He spoke so much about Christ," says Wiesel. "I was timid, but finally I said, 'You speak of Christ's suffering. What about the children who have suffered not 2,000 years ago, but yesterday? And they never talk about it." Mauriac was to recall the look in the speaker's pained eyes, "as of a Lazarus risen from the dead, yet still a prisoner within the grim confines where he had stayed, stumbling among the shameful corpses. . . . I could only embrace him weeping."

Four years later, *Night* appeared in France with an introduction by Mauriac. The little book set the Wiesel style: austere, tense phrases articu-

'Wiesel is a messenger to mankind; his message is one of peace, atonement and human dignity. His belief that the forces fighting evil in the world can be victorious is a hard-won belief.'

—THE NOBEL PRIZE COMMITTEE

lating the unspeakable—the murder and torture of the innocent, the martyrdom of faith itself as a child watches the hanging of another child: "'Where is God? Where is he?'... And I heard a voice within me answer: 'Where is he? Here he is—he is hanging here on this gallows.'"

Some 20 American publishers rejected *Night.* "The Holocaust was not something people wanted to know about in those days," the author remembers. "The diary of Anne Frank was about as far as anyone wanted to venture into the dark." *Night,* finally published in the U.S. in 1960, drew them far deeper, into an abyss that was appalling to contemplate and impossible to ignore. It was as if a thousand tongues had suddenly become unstuck.

Volumes by other writers, films, televisions programs followed *Night,* tracing the origins and consequences of genocide. Some of them were legitimate, but many were full of the now familiar Holocaust cant about survivor guilt or the complicity of the victims. Ironically, it was Wiesel who brought the term Holocaust out of scholarly usage into common parlance in a *New York Times* book review some 25 years ago: "I used it because I had no other word. Now I'm sorry. It's been so trivialized and vulgarized. Today one must ask, 'Do you mean the show or the event?'"

Yet despite the docudramas and paperback page turners with barbed wire on the covers, Wiesel has kept to his private tasks of organizing memory and troubling a deaf world with his cries. Although he has been called the voice of the 6 million killed in the "Final Solution," few of his more than 20 books directly confront the events of Auschwitz. Often they discuss the testamental prophets (*Five Biblical Portraits, Messengers of God*), ancient legend (*The Golem*) or contemporary Eastern Europe (*One Generation After*). His study of the Soviet Union (*The Jews of Silence*) was a new jeremiad, going beyond the crimes of the past. "People who didn't read the book thought it referred to the religious Russians no longer able to

'Open your doors. Open your gates. The gates of your heart. The doors of your memory... We must welcome refugees. They need refuge. We are their refuge.'

—ELIE WIESEL

'Just as despair can come to us only from other human beings, hope, too, can come to us only from other human beings.'

—ELIE WIESEL

study Hebrew or to pray in public," he says. "But what it really referred to was the American Jews who knew of the situation in the Soviet Union and said nothing. Indifference . . . it is something I know about." His grieving voice, marked with the intonations of the exile, trails off. "Silence is the worst thing, worse than mere hate. If we ignore the suffering, our true literary prophecy will not be *The Trial* or *The Stranger* but Hitler's *Mein Kampf.* This is what I fight against."

The battle has long since extended from Jewish themes to a concern for children everywhere. "The specter of starvation is not something consigned to the '30s and '40s," he says. "I look at the screen and see the swollen bellies and haunted eyes of the very young in Cambodia, in Ethiopia, in South America. I could have been that child. I was that child. And I must make a gesture."

Sometimes the gesture is a book, but often it is a journey to the side of the sufferers. Wiesel went to Cambodia to aid refugees and to Nicaragua to help the abused Miskito Indians. "I bring food," he says. "It is never enough, but to save one life is to save the world. And perhaps I can convince one other to save one more life."

It is here that the third title, teacher, is assumed. Of course, it could be argued that all of Wiesel's work is an attempt to instruct. But it is in his formal role as professor, first at City College in New York and then at Boston University, that Wiesel finds his profoundest satisfaction. "Had there been no war," he believes, "I would have been by now the head of a small school, instructing the young, unlocking the lessons of great texts. And today I am instructing the young, unlocking the lessons of great texts. Only these are different books: Kierkegaard, Kafka, Camus."

One book that the professor will never teach is Wiesel's *The Fifth Son.* Long ago, he decided never to analyze his own work, partly out of modesty ("They are for others to use, if the books are worthy") and partly out of the conviction that he has already coaxed the last possible meaning out of the sentences.

Wiesel, a former colleague of Camus's, has learned the lesson of the master. He animates his philosophy with incident and allows the moral to be implicit: If every suicide is a murder, every murder is a suicide, and revenge exacts a price that may be too exorbitant for God himself.

In Paris, where Wiesel has long been a best-selling author, *The Fifth Son* won the 1984 Grand Prize for Literature. For Wiesel, it was the latest of countless French awards, including Commander of the Legion of Honor, he has received other international tributes, and in the U.S. he has received some 20 honorary degrees. Twelve books have been devoted to a parsing of his life and works. And all of these pale beside an odd, unprecedented act in Germany. More than 70 delegates of the Bundestag wrote to the Nobel Prize Committee suggesting that Wiesel receive the 1985 Nobel Peace Prize for his work: "With great persuasion he has encouraged people around the world to reach a higher grade of moral sensitivity . . . It would be a great encouragement for all, among them the German people, who dedicate themselves to reconciliation." For almost any other candidate the suggestion could seem presumptuous. For Wiesel, it seems inevitable. For if the look of Lazarus has not left him, neither has the insatiable desire to rouse humanity from its self-concern.

In a book-clogged study on Manhattan's West Side, where he lives with his wife Marion, who translates his work from French into English, and their son Shlomo Elisha, Wiesel gazes down at the bare trees in Central Park and ponders. "Frequently I ask myself, how can one bring a child into this dreadful world, where Holocaust is now preceded by the word nuclear? And then I answer: In a faithless time, what greater act of belief is there than the one of birth? And what better thing to do than prevent the greatest murder of all: the killing of time."

'Elie Wiesel has created life out of death.'

— D.M. THOMAS

angela y. davis

by Joy James

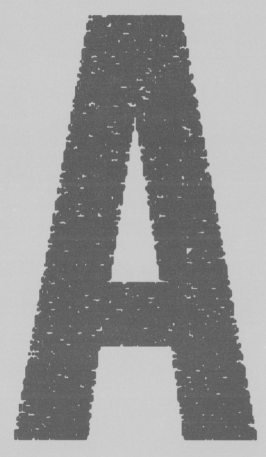

NGELA YVONNE DAVIS was born in Birmingham, Alabama, in 1944, near the close of the Second World War and the emergence of the United States as heir to British hegemony (a dominance which the US militarily retains, despite its slippage in the global economic and intellectual marketplace). She grew up in the Southern United States under Jim Crow segregation and codified racial discrimination. During the late 1940s, her family moved into a neighborhood that subsequently became known as "Dynamite Hill" because of Ku Klux Klan terrorism against black families being integrated into the previously all-white community. Although the Davis home was never targeted by white arsonists, houses across the street were bombed. Bombings and burnings continued for several years; "miraculously," recalls Davis, no one was killed.

Angela Y. Davis, born in Birmingham, Alabama, in 1944, was educated in France, the U.S., and Germany. A Communist activist, member of the Black Panther Party, and academic, she was on the FBI's most-wanted list for two months on charges of kidnapping. She was acquitted of all charges after spending 16 months in prison. Davis is currently professor at UC Santa Cruz, an author, and an activist in the prison-rights movement.

'It is important not only to have the awareness and to feel impelled to become involved, it's important that there be a forum out there to which one can relate, an organization, a movement.'

— ANGELA DAVIS

Racial segregation had created an apartheid-like Southern US in which African-American students, regardless of their economic status, usually attended the same (underfunded) schools. As a child, Davis was considered part of an elite among impoverished peers. Because of her family's financial security and the extreme poverty of some classmates, the grade schooler stole from her father, giving money to children to buy their school lunch. Partly to escape the social roles defined by her middle-class standing in the black community and the educational limitations of local schools bound by Jim Crow and inequitable state funding, Davis left the South in 1959, for Manhattan, New York, where, under the auspices of a Quaker educational program, she lived with a progressive white family and attended a private high school, Elizabeth Irwin/Little Red School House. There she studied Karl Marx and Frederick Engel's *The Communist Manifesto*, and at age fifteen became active in a youth organization associated with the Communist Party. . . .

Upon high school graduation and with a scholarship in hand, Davis left New York to attend Brandeis University in Massachusetts; she studied there with philosopher Herbert Marcuse, and took her junior year in France at the Sorbonne. This was the height of the civil rights movement emanating from the 1955 Montgomery, Alabama, bus boycotts that had established US apartheid.

Terrorist assaults against black activists provided the radicalizing impetus to end her European studies in the late 1960s. In fact, the racist murders of childhood acquaintances in her hometown during her first study abroad, in the early 1960s, profoundly affected her. In both the autobiography and a 1993 essay, "Remembering Carole, Cynthia, Addie Mae and Denise," Davis recounts how, while in France, she learned of the September 15, 1963, bombing of Birmingham's Sixteenth Street Baptist Church. In that foray by white extremists, fourteen-year-olds Carole Robertson, Cynthia Wesley, and Addie Mae Collins, and eleven-year-old

Denise McNair, died. The bombing occurred soon after the historic 1963 March on Washington, DC, and Martin Luther King Jr's eschatological "I Have a Dream" speech. Davis reminisces that declining the scholarship to the private school in Manhattan would have probably placed her nearby at Fisk University in Nashville, Tennessee, at the time of the bombing. It was during her stay in Europe, far from family ties and a society schooled in sur-viving and confronting white violence, that Davis learned of, and became deeply disturbed by, the girls' deaths: "If I had not been in France, news would not have been broken to me about the deaths. . . I was in Biarritz, liv-ing among people so far removed from the civil-rights war unfolding in the South that it made little sense to try to express to them how devastated I felt. I wrestled in solitude with my grief, my fear and my rage."

The search for human liberation greater than the US Constitution's promise of electoral powers led Angela Davis to the Black Panther Party for Self-Defense. Davis became a member of the Communist Party USA in 1968, at the same time that she joined the Panthers; however, her ties with the CPUSA proved less problematic than her relationship with the BPP. Her affiliation with the Panthers would last less than two years; with the Communist Party, it would endure for over twenty. Initially Davis joined the CPUSA because of her commitments to internationalist struggle. Like W.E.B. Du Bois, who after the Second World War, began to incorporate Marxist theory into his analysis of oppression, Davis felt that black libera-tion was unobtainable apart from an international workers' movement against capitalism, imperialism, and racism. Her understanding that a mass liberation struggle needed to be class-based in order to confront the racist foundations of capitalism was strengthened by a 1969 trip to Cuba.

Davis's political work and personal life within organizations such as the Communist Party and the Black Panther Party made her vulnerable to attacks by university administrations. By 1969, the new assistant phi-

'I want to suggest that particularly at this time in the history of our country and the history of the globe, radical activism is needed more than ever before and that women and women's issues need to be at the forefront in this radical activism.'

— ANGELA DAVIS

losophy professor at the University of California at Los Angeles (UCLA) was recognized in the state as a radical antiracist and a Communist.

Despite the professional costs, she openly served for twenty-three years in active leadership on the Party's Central Committee and twice ran for Vice-President on its national ticket.

Active in the Communist Party, Davis became engaged in prisoners' rights activism during the time that she was defending her right to teach at UCLA. Her organizing focused on a mass defense for the Soledad Brothers: George Jackson, Fleeta Drumgo, and John Clutchette.

To publicize prison conditions and state abuses against the Soledad Brothers, and out of love for his brother, George, in August 1970, Jonathan Jackson, a member of Davis's security, carried guns into a courtroom in northern Marin County. With prisoners James McClain, William Christmas, and Ruchell Magee, he took as hostages the judge, district attorney, and several members of the jury. The high school student and inmates brought the hostages to a van in the parking lot. San Quentin guards fired on the parked vehicle, killing Judge Haley, Jonathan Jackson, and prisoners McCain and Christmas, while seriously wounding the district attorney, several jurors, and prisoner Magee who later became Davis's codefendant. She was not in northern California at the time, but because the guns were registered in her name, Davis was named by police as an accomplice. In that era, at the height of the FBI's counterintelligence program to undermine the civil rights and black liberation movements—police, assisted by federal agents, had killed or assassinated over twenty black revolutionaries in the Black Panther Party. Rather than turn herself in to the authorities, Davis went underground and for two months was on the Federal Bureau of Investigation's "Ten Most Wanted List." Captured in Manhattan on October 13, 1970, she would spend the next sixteen months in prison, most of it in solitary confinement, before her release on bail.

'The quest for the emancipation of black people in the US has always been a quest for economic liberation which means to a certain extent that the rise of black middle class would be inevitable'

— ANGELA DAVIS

On January 5, 1971, in *The People of the State of California vs. Angela Y. Davis*, the state arraigned Angela Davis in a small Marin County Courtroom on charges of murder, kidnapping, and conspiracy.

In February 1972, after intense and lengthy lobbying by activists to end dehumanizing prison conditions and judicial racism in sentencing, the state Supreme Court abolished the death penalty in California, a decision that would facilitate Davis's release on bail. The trial, which progressed throughout 1971 and into the following year, ended just as the Soledad Brothers' trial had: Angela Yvonne Davis was acquitted of all charges when the jury rendered its "not guilty" verdict on June 4, 1972.

Although she had written extensively for nearly thirty years as a radical intellectual, Davis remains best known as a representational figure of a revolutionary movement in US domestic racial politics.

Within the context of a past liberation movement, a younger Davis had offered insights into revolutionary liberation in the 1970 *LIFE* Magazine profile published while she was underground. *LIFE*'s cover superimposed the caption "The Making of a Fugitive" over her photograph, while the feature article reprinted the following quote taken from one of Davis's speeches for the Soledad Brothers:

> Liberation is synonymous with revolution. . . . A revolution is not just armed struggle. It's not just the period in which you can take over. A revolution has a very, very long spectrum. . . . Che made the very important point that the society you're going to build is already reflected in the nature of the struggle that you're carrying out. And one of the most important things in relationship to that is the building of a collective spirit, getting away from this individualistic orientation towards personal salvation, personal involvement. . . . One of the most important things that has to be done in the process of carrying out a revolutionary struggle is to merge those two different levels, to merge the personal with the political where they're no longer separate.

'Reagan vowed that Davis would never teach in the University of California school system again. Today Davis is the first African-American to hold a tenured professorship at the U of C at Santa Cruz.'

— TRACY DEUTMEYER

mohandas k. gandhi

by Thomas Merton

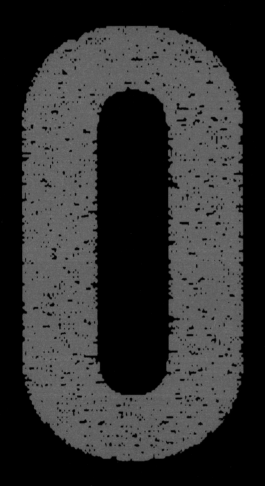

ONE OF THE MOST SIGNIFICANT FACTS ABOUT the life and vocation of Gandhi was his discovery of the East through the West. Like so many others of India, Gandhi received a completely Western education as a young man. He had to a great extent renounced the beliefs, the traditions, the habits of thought, of India. He spoke, thought, and acted like an Englishman, except of course that an Englishman was precisely what he could never, by any miracle, become. He was an alienated Asian whose sole function in life was to be perfectly English without being English at all: to prove the superiority of the West by betraying his own heritage and his own self, thinking as a white man without ceasing to be "a Nigger." The beauty of this (at least to Western minds) was that it showed Western culture to be a pearl of such great price that one could rea-

Mohandas K. Gandhi **was born in India in 1869, studied law in London, and spent 20 years in South Africa. In 1914 he returned to India, becoming a leader in the Indian National Congress and supporting the movement for Home Rule. Known for his non-violent means of rebellion, and his part in negotiating the Indian independence in 1947, he was killed by an extremist for his work on the Hindu-Muslim conflict.**

'Generations to come will scarce believe that such a one as this ever in flesh and blood walked upon this earth.'

—ALBERT EINSTEIN

sonably sell the whole of Asia in order to acquire it, even though the acquisition was not that of a new being, or even of a new identity, but only of a new suit.

Gandhi was unusual in this. Instead of being fooled by the Western costume, and instead of being persuaded that he no longer really existed as an Asian, he recognized that the West had something good about it that was good not because it was Western but because it was also Eastern: that is to say, it was *universal.* So he turned his face and heart once again to India, and saw what was really there. It was through his acquaintance with writers like Tolstoy and Thoreau, and then his reading of the New Testament, that Gandhi rediscovered his own tradition and his Hindu *dharma* (religion, duty). More than a tradition, more than a wisdom handed down in books or celebrated in temples, Gandhi discovered India in discovering himself. Hence it is very important indeed to understand Gandhi's political life, and particularly his non-violence, in light of this radical discovery from which everything else received its meaning. Gandhi's dedicated struggle for Indian freedom and his insistence on non-violent means in the struggle— both resulted from his new understanding of India and of himself after his contact with a *universally valid* spiritual tradition which he saw to be common to both East and West. . . .

In rediscovering India and his own "right mind," Gandhi was not excavating from libraries the obscure disputed questions of Vedantic scholasticism (though he did not reject Vedanta). He was, on the contrary, identifying himself fully with the Indian people, that is to say not with the Westernized upper classes nor with the Brahmin caste, but rather with the starving masses and in particular with the outcaste "untouchables," or *Harijan.*

This again is a supremely important fact, without which Gandhi's non-violence is incomprehensible. The awakening of the Indian mind in

Gandhi was not simply the awakening of his own spirit to the possibilities of a distinctly Hindu form of "interior life." It was not just a question of Yoga *asanas* and Vedantic spiritual disciplines for his own perfection. Gandhi realized that *the people of India were awakening in him.* The masses who had been totally silent for thousands of years had now found a voice in him. It was not "Indian thought" or "Indian spirituality" that was stirring in him, but India herself. It was the spiritual consciousness of a people that awakened in the spirit of one person. But the message of the Indian spirit, of Indian wisdom, was not for India alone. It was for the entire world. Hence Gandhi's message was valid for India and for himself in so far as it represented *the awakening of a new world.*

Yet this renewed spiritual consciousness of India was entirely different from the totalitarian and nationalist consciousness that came alive in the West and in the East (Japan) to the point of furious and warlike vitality. The Indian mind that was awakening in Gandhi was inclusive not exclusive. It was at once Indian and universal. It was not a mind of hate, of intolerance, of accusation, of rejection, of division. It was a mind of love, of understanding, of infinite capriciousness. Where the extreme nationalisms of Western Fascism and of Japan were symptoms of paranoid fury, exploding into alienation, division, and destruction, the spirit which Gandhi discovered in himself was reaching out to unity, love, and peace. It was a spirit which was, he believed, strong enough to heal every division.

In Gandhi's mind, non-violence was not simply a political tactic which was supremely useful and efficacious in liberating his people from foreign rule, in order that India might then concentrate on realizing its own national identity. On the contrary, the spirit of non-violence sprang from *an inner realization of spiritual unity in himself.* The whole Gandhian concept of non-violent action and satyagraha is incomprehensible if it is thought to be a means of achieving unity rather than as *the fruit of inner unity already achieved.*

> '**Non-violence is the greatest force at the disposal of mankind. It is mightier than the mightiest weapon of destruction devised by the ingenuity of man.**'
>
> —MOHANDAS K. GANDHI

All the political acts of Gandhi were, then, at the same time spiritual and religious acts in fulfillment of the Hindu *dharma*. They were meaningful on at least three different levels at once: first as acts of religious worship, second as symbolic and educative acts bringing the Indian people to a realization of their true needs and their place in the life of the world, and finally they had a universal import as manifestations of urgent truths, the unmasking of political falsehood, awakening all men to the demands of the time and to the need for renewal and unity on a world scale.

In Gandhi the voice of Asia, not the Asia of the Vedas and Sutras only, but the Asia of the hungry and silent masses, was speaking and still speaks to the whole world with a prophetic message. This message, uttered on dusty Indian roads, remains more meaningful than those specious promises that have come from the great capitals of the earth. As Father Monchanin, the French priest and scholar who became a hermit in India, declared at Gandhi's death: "When we hear the voice of Gandhi we hear the voice of his Mother [India] and of his nurse. We hear the voice of all the peasant masses bending over the rice fields of India."

"Man cannot be free if he does not know that he is subject to necessity, because his freedom is always won in his never wholly successful attempts to liberate himself from necessity."

We have seen that Gandhi's political philosophy was based on this principle, because his religious intuition of the Hindu dharma saw all life as one in a sacred cosmic family in which each member helped to elevate the whole from a selfish and destructive to a spiritual and productive level through sacrificial participation in the common needs and struggles of all. Hence the cornerstone of all Gandhi's life, action, and thought was the respect for the sacredness of life and the conviction that "love is the law of our being." For he said, "If love or non-violence be not the law of our being, the whole of my argument falls to pieces." Note he also says that "Truth is

'Gandhi's ideas have applications wherever there are poor, oppressed people—even in the richest country in the world, as has been demonstrated by Martin Luther King, Jr., and Cesar Chavez.'

—VED MEHTA

the law of our being." But obviously Gandhi's life was without meaning unless we take into account the fact that it was lived in the face of untruth and hatred, the persistent and flagrant denial of love.

Sometimes the idea of non-violence is taken to be the result of a purely sentimental evasion of unpleasant reality. Foggy clichés about Oriental metaphysics leave complacent Westerners with the idea that for the East (and as everyone knows, the Easterners are all "quietists" besides being "enigmatic") nothing really exists anyway. All is illusion, and suffering itself is illusion. Non-violence becomes a way of "making violence stop" by sitting down in front of it and wishing it was not there. This, together with the refusal to eat meat or kill ants, indeed even mosquitoes, is supposedly thought to create an aura of benevolence which may effectively inhibit the violence of Englishmen (who are in any case kind to dogs, etc.) but cannot be expected to work against Nazis and Russians. So much for Western evaluations!

Gandhi knew the reality of hatred and untruth because he had felt them in his own flesh: indeed he succumbed to them when he was assassinated on January 30, 1948. Gandhi's non-violence was therefore not a sentimental evasion or denial of the reality of evil. It was a clear-sighted acceptance of the necessity to use the force and the presence of evil as a fulcrum for good and for liberation. . . .

Peace cannot be built on exclusivism, absolutism, and intolerance. But neither can it be built on vague liberal slogans and pious programs gestated in the smoke of confabulation. There can be no peace on earth without the kind of inner change that brings man back to his "right mind."

'If humanity is to progress, Gandhi is inescapable. He lived, thought and acted, inspired by the vision of humanity evolving toward a world of peace and harmony. We may ignore Gandhi at our own risk.'

—MARTIN LUTHER KING, JR.

acknowledgments

Allende excerpt from "Death and Rebirth in Chile" by Ariel Dorfman, *The Nation* 10/8/90 . ©1990 Reprinted by permission of The Nation. Photograph ©Archive Photos/PNI.

Bull excerpt from "Living in Our Own Fashion" by Geoffrey C. Ward, *American Heritage Magazine* 9/93. Reprinted by permission of American Heritage Magazine, a division of Forbes, Inc. ©1993 Forbes, Inc. Photograph ©UPI/Corbis-Bettmann.

Brown excerpt from *John Brown: A Biography* by W.E.B. DuBois ©1962 W.E.B. DuBois. Reprinted by permission of International Publishers. Photograph ©UPI/Corbis-Bettmann.

Castro excerpt from *A Personal Portrait of Fidel* by Gabriel García Márquez. ©1998 by Fidel Castro. Reprinted by permission of Ocean Press. Photograph ©Archive Photos.

Chavez excerpt from "Cesar Chavez" by Peter Matthiesson, *The New Yorker* 6/21/69 ©1969 Reprinted by permission of Peter Matthiesson. Photograph ©Archive Photos/PNI.

Collins excerpt from *Michael Collins: The Man Who Made Ireland* by Tim Pat Coogan. ©1992, 1996 by Tim Pat Coogan. Reprinted by permission of Roberts Rinehart Publishing. Photograph ©UPI/Corbis-Bettmann.

Davis excerpt from *The Angela Y. Davis Reader* by Joy James ©1998 Joy James. Reprinted by permission of Blackwell Publishers Ltd. Photograph ©Archive Photos/PNI.

Gandhi excerpt from *Gandhi and the One-Eyed Giant* by Thomas Merton ©1964, 1965 by New Directions Publishing Corp. Reprinted by permission of New Directions Publishing Corp. Photograph ©Archive Photos/PNI.

Guevara excerpt from *Fidel Castro's Oct. 18, 1967, Tribute to Che Guevara* by Fidel Castro ©1967 Reprinted by permission of Pathfinder Press. Photograph ©Archive Photos/PNI

Havel excerpt from "Saluting the Playwright Who Became President" by Peter C. Newman, *Maclean's* 8/17/98 ©1998 Reprinted by permission of Peter C. Newman. Photograph ©Archive Photos/PNI.

Kyi excerpt from "Lady in Waiting" by Anna Husarska, *The New Republic* 4/12/99 ©1999 Reprinted by permission of The New Republic, Inc. Photograph ©Robin Moyer.

Lama excerpt from "God in Exile" by Pico Iyer. *Time* 12/22/97. ©1997 Reprinted by permission of Time, Inc. Photograph ©Archive Photos/PNI

Lorca excerpt from "Poets and Politics" by González Echevarría, *The New York Times* 9/12/99. ©1999 Reprinted by permission of *The New York Times*. Photograph ©Archive Photos

Luxemburg excerpt from *Reflections on Rosa* by Stephen Eric Bronner. ©1978 Reprinted by permission of Westview Press, Inc. Photograph ©UPI/Corbis-Bettmann.

Mandela excerpt from "Nelson Mandela" by André Brink. *Time* 4/13/98. ©1998 Reprinted by permission of Time, Inc. Photograph ©SYGMA

Marcos excerpt from "The Unmasking" by Alma Guillermoprieto *The New Yorker* 3/13/95. ©1995 Reprinted by permission of Alma Guillermoprieto and the Watkins/Loomis Agency. Photograph ©Eniac Martínez.

Minh excerpt from *Ho* by David Halberstam. ©1986 by David Halberstam. Reprinted by permission of Mc Graw Hill College Division. Photograph ©Archive Photos/PNI.

Perón excerpt from *The Return of Eva Perón with the Killings in Trinidad* by V.S. Naipaul. ©1980 by V.S. Naipaul. Reprinted by permission of Alfred A. Knopf, a Division of Random House, Inc. Photograph ©UPI/Corbis-Bettmann.

Solzhenitsyn excerpt from "Solzhenitsyn's History Lesson" by Nina Khrushcheva. *The Nation* 5/3/99 ©1999 Reprinted by permission of The Nation. Photograph ©Archive Photos.

Stanton excerpt from "Elizabeth Cady Stanton" from *Portraits of American Women: From Settlement to the Present* by Bruce Miroff. ©1998 Reprinted by permission of Catherine Clinton & Barker-Benfield? Photograph ©UPI/Corbis-Bettmann.

Tubman excerpt from "Bound to Freedom" by Andrew Porter *U.S. News & World Report* 4/14/97 ©1997 Reprinted by permission of U.S. News & World Report. Photograph ©Archive Photos/PNI.

Villa excerpt from *The Life and Times of Pancho Villa* by Friedrich Katz with the permission of the publishers, Stanford University Press. ©1998 Board of Trustees of the Leland Stanford Junior University. Photograph ©Archive Photos/PNI.

Walesa excerpt from *Righteous Gentile* by John Bierman ©1981 by John Bierman. Reprinted by permission of Viking Press. Photograph ©Archive Photos/PNI.

Wiesel excerpt from "Books: Author, Teacher, Witness" by Stefan Kanfer, *Time* 3/18/85. ©1985 Reprinted by permission of Time, Inc. Photograph ©Archive Photos.

Malcolm X excerpt from "Alex Haley Remembers" *from The Man, The Myth, and the Mission* by Alex Haley. ©1992 by David Gallen. Reprinted by permission of Ballentine Books. Photograph ©Archive Photos/PNI.